SPARKS AT SEA

SPARKS AT SEA

The Experiences of a Ship's Radio Officer

R. W. Chandler

David & Charles: Newton Abbot

0 7153 5953 3

Set in 11/13 Baskerville
and printed in Great Britain
by W. J. Holman Limited Dawlish
for David & Charles (Publishers) Limited
South Devon House Newton Abbot Devon

For Susan Wilson, whose help and
patience have contributed so much

I acknowledge with thanks the invaluable
assistance given me by Mr Craig, J. M.
Carter of the *Journal of Commerce* and
editor of *Sea Breezes*, and Edmund R. Newman
of Ellerman Lines Ltd.

Contents

CHAPTER ONE

Training & My First Ship

I WOULD like to recall that I did something dramatic as I stepped on board my first ship the *City of Marseilles*—that I paused, took off my cap, and swore to be worthy of my calling—but I was so busy trying to follow the two lascars carrying my baggage that I just scuttled across the littered iron deck and down a ladder, and then down another ladder, until I was stopped by a cabin door. It was being unlocked by another lascar. He wore blue dungarees and a small white hat, and had bare feet. 'Me boy', he said simply and opened the door. My first sea home had two bunks on one bulkhead, and a round porthole in the other, below which was a settee. At the foot of the settee was a wash basin. The boy pointed to the bottom bunk. 'Him yours', he said. I pointed to the top bunk and the boy smiled. 'You only man.' He waved a thin black hand around the tiny white painted room. 'All yours, Now I show you radio room.' I followed him back up the two ladders to the cluttered deck, where he unlocked the door of a square iron house and waved me in. The radio room was about 8ft square, a sound-proofed cabin containing in one corner a rotary spark gap transmitter, and, on a bench across the after-facing bulkhead, the radio receiver with a chair in front of it. I had a small feeling of comfort because the transmitter and receiver were types I had been trained on. 'I now get Sahib's tea', said the boy. I sat down in the chair, and wondered how I had got that far.

From the age of ten I knew I was going to sea; nobody put the idea into my head, I think I grew up with it.

We lived in the middle of Norfolk, 50 miles from the coast, and my father was the engineer on a country estate—an important position in the 1920s, when the country gentry, in order to have the comforts becoming common in the cities, installed their own electric generating plant, water-pumping stations and other temperamental gadgetry requiring an expert to keep it functioning. True, my father had been in the Navy for twenty years before being invalided out after an accident, but he never tried to influence me and didn't even talk about his life at sea.

So at sixteen I left grammar school, bored with prayers and the sports field. There was no chance of going to sea as an apprentice deck officer, because I had worn spectacles since childhood. To be a ship's engineer I had to serve an apprenticeship in a shipyard or engineering works, and such places did not exist in the middle of Norfolk. I considered becoming a chief steward or purser, but the former position seemed only attainable by starting as a galley boy and climbing a long ladder of promotion, and pursers were appointed from the head offices of the shipowners. For a time I turned over a suggestion that writers in the Navy did not need top-grade eyesight, but to a boy of sixteen joining the Navy didn't seem to be going to sea; and the likelihood of remaining at anchor for weeks at a time, combined with the total lack of privacy of the mess decks and rigid discipline reminded me too much of school.

It was about this time that I found out about the *Journal of Commerce*, which showed me the ships that really went to sea—the deep-sea tramps of the late 1920s—and following their wanderings week by week became a fascinating hobby. The *Baron Tweedmouth*, Barry to Santa Fé with coal, then from Rosario to Manila with maize, and from Iloilo to Boston with sugar. Dozens of them wandered the seven seas where cargo was available and offered. These to my mind were the true seafarers.

One issue of the *Journal* had an advertisement that showed me the way to my ambition—to become a marine wireless operator. Perfect eyesight was not required and the job carried the status of a junior officer, which meant that in most ships he had a cabin to himself or, at worst, shared a cabin with another radio operator, and that he had his meals in the saloon. So, of necessity, it was decided that I would become a marine radio operator, a title later changed to radio officer.

A letter of enquiry to the British School of Wireless Telegraphy produced a most comprehensive brochure, which explained just how to obtain the necessary Postmaster General licence and what the career chances were when you had obtained one. It was necessary to reach a speed of fifteen words a minute receiving and sending in morse code groups and twenty-five words a minute in plain language. There were two written papers—one on electricity and magnetism and one on advanced radio. There was also an oral examination followed by a practical test of finding faults on a complete ship's radio installation. In the opinion of the British School of Telegraphy this meant at least one year in the school. This was a very fair assessment; one brilliant youth managed it in nine months but the general run of students took between one year and sixteen months to obtain the licence. An aunt who lived in London agreed to supply me with a home during my period at school, I was allocated a small weekly sum for pocket money and fares, and bright and early one morning I presented myself at 198 Stockwell Road, London, the home of the British School of Wireless Telegraphy.

This was a typical Victorian three-storey London house. The large rooms on the first two storeys were filled with morse keys and headphones, and in the garden at the back were two lecture rooms and a wooden shed fitted up to represent a ship's radio room. The students came from all over England and mostly from middle-class families. We soon settled down to learning and then practising the morse code, and within a month I found that the magic fifteen words a minute code and twenty-five words a minute plain language were going to call for a lot of intensive practice. I felt sure that the theory and practical application of radio could be assimilated in the year, but those fantastic speeds seemed well out of my reach.

During the first few months the natural leaders began to emerge and take their places, but, in contrast to the grammar school, they were those who worked the hardest. We all came from families that had made considerable sacrifices to send us to the school for a year, and the shirkers soon became despised and dropped out. There was no strong 'honour of the school' feeling or any traditions to be upheld; we were all concerned in obtaining the necessary licence within the year and our main interest was finding out what sort of a career would be open to us when this magic document was obtained. A few of the students, still imbued with the school spirit, started cricket and football teams, but these died in turn from lack of support. After a grammar school life, the BSWT was probably the best place for showing that powers on the sports field or attendance at church parades did not necessarily help in earning one's living. The leaders of our course emerged because they were people who had already been at sea in different minor capacities and had decided that radio-operating offered better chances of advancement than the occupation they had first chosen. They emerged because they knew so much more than the rest of us what this business of going to sea really meant.

One of them had been a bellboy for a year in a P&O Company liner where his education in the seamy side of life had been considerable. Another had been a galley boy and later a junior steward in an old liner, and his stories of the filth and squalor of the 'glory hole', as he called the stewards' accommodation, were indeed hard to accept; though I was later to find that they were most probably true. Another had been an apprentice with a South Wales tramp-ship company, but his eyesight had failed before his apprenticeship was complete. His was an accurate story of the life in that class of ship; the only thing I couldn't believe was that the food was as unbelievably bad as he said it was, but I was to find later that he was right. A fourth student had been at sea as what was known in those days as a watcher: he was taught enough to recognise the SOS sign, at which point he called the real operator. There seemed to be three watchers on the frozen-meat boat he was on, and, when they were not watching, they were sailors. Watchers had been displaced by automatic equipment by the time I got to sea, but it must have been a job in which loyalties were divided between the mate and the radio operator. At the break periods these four students would be surrounded by a mob of us listening to their stories open-mouthed. I think we all rejected the unpleasant and believed the pleasant, because we were all going to sea anyway and we could not possibly have chosen the wrong road.

The students varied in age from sixteen to thirty and came from all sorts of occupations. One was a charabanc driver, who had no intention of going to sea but had been sent to the school by his father 'to make something of himself'. He failed to, and before the course finished he was back driving his charabanc. Another student, who was in his middle twenties and came from Jersey, was the quietest man I have ever met: he never discussed his home, job, anything, but he got his licence at the end of the course with ease. He could talk, evidently, because on his first trip to sea as third operator on a P&O boat he managed to get the daughter of a civil servant en route to Borneo in the family way and then talked his way into a job out there in the telegraph system as a condition for making the lady his wife.

Another student appeared a complete misfit. His father, an Italian, kept a restaurant in the East End of London, and his son looked and dressed the part of an Italian opera singer. 'Poppa', as he called his father, insisted that his son go to sea. Tonelli, for that was his name, had no intention of going to sea, since his father paid his waiters better money than he could earn there, but strangely enough he did go. Years later, lying alongside a jetty in the East River, I watched a smart white American cruise liner warped alongside ahead of us and thought I recognised Tonelli on the bridge rails. When she was alongside, I went aboard and it was Tonelli—bigger, more confident, and chief operator of that cruise liner, complete with a wife and family and American citizenship. He bore little resemblance to the little Italian who had learnt his morse code with me. He wined me and dined me in the ship's saloon, and then I went back to the rust-streaked, hungry gutted, old British tramp of which I was also the chief, but only, radio operator. Another student I remember well was considered by the rest of us to be hopeless. George could play his banjo for us in the break periods but was a dead loss at radio. He failed to obtain his licence, but five years later became a bandleader whose name was a household word.

Some students found the morse code simple, but I found it difficult, and for months seemed to lag behind the others. It took me years to attain the standard where it became a second language to me. Over the years I was to meet people whose ability to send and receive the morse code was amazing. One man was really uncanny. He had been twenty years on liners on the North Atlantic and had trained himself to be a touch typist. I have watched him receive a long press report by storing up thirty or forty words in his memory and then typing it in short bursts, complete with capital letters and punctuation—and the press would be coming over at about twenty-five words a minute. I watched him one night eating his sandwiches and later rolling a cigarette between his short bursts on the typewriter.

The PMG examinations were getting nearer and tension was mounting. Theoretically and practically, I was confident of success, but this damnable morse-code speed just wouldn't come. Fate was on my side, however. On the Saturday afternoon before the examinations, which started on the Monday, I smashed the two fingers of my left hand playing cricket for a youth club I had joined. I went through the motions of sitting for the examination but failed it in every part, and was told to try again in three months. I managed to keep my fingers out of trouble when the next examinations came round and passed easily.

Three months later a registered letter arrived containing a document that authorised me to operate radio-telegraph equipment on a ship. I applied for a position in this capacity with a large company that rented out ships' radio equipment and supplied personnel to operate it, and after some weeks I was called to London for an interview and was accepted. Enclosed with the letter of appointment was a list of uniforms I would need for my new job, and that necessitated two more trips to London. Finally I sent a letter to the radio company to say that I was all fitted out and ready to go.

Now started the longest two weeks of my life, I read the shipping *Journal* from cover to cover, paying special attention to the movements of liners in and out of London. I knew I would start on a liner and was convinced I would sail from London. I tried on my uniform with the single wavy stripe on the cuff a dozen times, packed and repacked my bags, but didn't quite pluck up the courage to cycle round the Norfolk countryside in my new regalia—much as I would have liked to. The magic summons came to report to the company's Southampton office at 9.30 the next Monday morning. The last few copies of the shipping *Journal* were at once studied for liners sailing on Monday or Tuesday, but there was only one, a Union Castle liner, and that company employed its own radio operators. I made the journey from Norfolk to Southampton resplendent in my new uniform and presented myself on the radio company's doorstep at 9.0am on the great day.

A completely disinterested clerk eventually pointed to a scruffy waiting room and said: 'Just stick around, you will be called when we want you'. There were several nondescript men sitting around, but no one took the slightest notice of me for at least two hours, until a large man with a bowler hat perched on the back of his head and smelling very strongly of stale beer plonked himself down beside me. He gazed moodily at my new uniform and then in a voice like a foghorn said: 'Phwat have we here then? A first tripper by all that's holy; would yew be from the ould country an all?' I explained where I came from but my Irish friend only laughed. 'Ye can't all be as lucky as me. I'll bet you're just bustin' of questions and no one to ask 'em of; you go ahead.' I asked who the waiting men were. 'Me bhoy, all good members of the union; the ones with the long faces are signing on this day for ships on long voyages to distant parts. The ones with smart clothes and ties an' all, they're for the big ships.'

'What will happen to me then?' I asked. Paddy replied quietly: 'You'll sign on as third man on one of the big ships; don't worry none about it, you'll get used to it when you get over the sickness if you are unlucky enough to get that'. No one had taken any notice of me and I pointed this out to my new found friend. 'Don't worry, dat one behind the counter is the staff clerk; he knows you're here and what ship he is going to send you to, but he won't be telling you until he's good and ready.' He pointed to a redfaced man who was working behind the counter in the corner. 'Staff clerks are mighty important people; get on their wrong side and they'll shanghai you on to some old tramp where you won't get a decent meal in a two years' articles. Some of them are liable to take a little sweetening to assist them in selecting your next ship', he said, 'but that won't worry you until you have three years' sea time in and you are allowed to go to sea on your own.'

The redfaced man behind the counter leaned forward. 'You', he grated, pointing a grubby finger in my direction. I scrambled to my feet and up to the counter. 'You're going as No 2 in the *City of Marseilles*, signing on at 2 o'clock this afternoon. The No 1 is on leave and won't be back until Thursday.' He shoved some papers into my hands and turned away. Paddy now became a tower of strength. He examined the papers. 'No 2 on the *City of Marseilles*, eh', he grunted. 'She's a trooper, signing on in the shipping office at 2.0pm.' He looked at me with a twinkle in his eye. 'You don't even know where that is, do you?' He heaved himself to his feet and marched firmly up to the staff clerk's counter; the clerk backed off, saying: 'Haven't anything for you at the moment'.

'Fine', said Paddy. 'You won't mind if I show this lad where his ship is and where the shipping office is, will you?' His breath was too much for the staff clerk. 'Help yourself', he said.

Paddy now took complete control; he ushered me straight into the saloon bar of the nearest pub and bought me half a pint of mild. 'Start on this stuff, if you haven't had a drink before', he counselled, and promptly downed a pint of draught Guinness. All my resolutions about being a teetotaller and saving my money were forgotten; but the first sip of the mild beer was horrible, and I made a mental note that if I was going to become an alcoholic I should have to find something more palatable to drink. Paddy waved my offer of another Guinness aside. 'I am just back from a fifteen month trip', he laughed, and proceeded to demolish no less than six more pints of Guinness. He talked steadily, ordering steak and kidney pies for us to eat at a table in the bar and continuing to talk while we ate them. In two hours he told me a lot about being a radio operator at sea. He told me that the merchant navy did not wear their uniforms ashore; that I was entitled to bedding, towels, and having my cabin cleaned up; and a dozen things that were to help so much later.

At 2 o'clock he took me into a large building that he explained was the shipping office, 'where you signed on the ship's articles before you sailed and signed off when the voyage was complete'. I presented my papers to a man behind a grill on Paddy's instruction; he read them, swung a large book round and pointed: 'Sign there'. I did and became the second radio officer of His Majesty's Transport *City of Marseilles*. I walked across the large dirty room to where Paddy was sprawling on a hard form. 'Well that's it, ould son. Where's your gear then?'

I explained that it was booked in the Southampton railway station. 'There's a taxi driver around here sometimes; used to be a radio man until he took to wimmin and gave up the business. Let's find him.' Paddy found his friend's cab outside a dubious looking club. 'Wait here now. I'll just join Mr Powell and let him buy me a glass of something for finding him a customer.' They arrived at the cab in about twenty minutes. Paddy's friend was another Irishman, who greeted me cheerfully: 'Hop in, ould son. We'll do this job before that Orangeman bum you picked up wants me to buy him more strong drink on the strength of your fare.' 'An' it's married you claim you are', replied Paddy. 'That poor girl sees less of your money than if you'd stayed at sea; you spend more time in pubs than is right at all.' Paddy turned to me. 'Good luck, me bhoy. I'll be off back to that office and see phwat that man has saved up for me.' He rolled off down the pavement, his good deed done, and we never met again. I never even heard his name.

The cabbie soon had me at the station and my bags loaded. 'Don't think about it, son.' He must have noted my last look after the departing Paddy. 'We all had to make our first trip; leave it to me—the *City of Marseilles*, is it?' he said as we threaded our way through the streets of Southampton. 'One of the Ellerman City Line, Scotch officers and a lascar crew. I did a trip in their *City of Paris* once. The food was good.' Suddenly he pointed. 'That's her across the dock there', and I gazed at my first ship. To me she appeared huge—white-painted with a blue band round the hull and a single buff funnel. Then we drew alongside the gangway. 'Sit tight', said my new mentor. 'I'll find your boy.' In a few minutes he returned followed by two lascars who grabbed my baggage and climbed up to the deck. The cabdriver accepted one of my last pound notes with the remark: 'Just follow those two, they will know where your cabin is, and have a good trip.'

Thus did I find the *City of Marseilles*.

CHAPTER TWO

The City of Marseilles, Hong Kong, Bombay

THE second radio officer, complete with his single wavy stripe, was now very much aboard. I studied the papers that had been pushed into my hands by the staff clerk and found that my salary was £7 7s 0d (£7.35) per month and that I had signed on for a two-year voyage at 1s a month. In any one calendar month the shipowner could advance me the sum of £4. My cogitations were interrupted by the return of the boy with a tray of toast, tea and cakes. Paddy's steak and kidney pie was just a memory by this time and I demolished the lot. I then went down to the cabin and stowed away my gear, and, while I was doing this and admiring the set of my new cap, the boy returned, saying: 'Supper ready, Sahib. You come now. I show you'. Back on deck again and then into a long alleyway that led into a large room with a high domed ceiling —the saloon. It was filled with tables and chairs, but only over one table in the corner were lights burning. The boy led me across to this table and revolved one of the chairs, which were secured to the floor. I sat down.

The only other occupant was a baldheaded middleaged man who gave me a pleasant smile. 'First trip, laddie?' he asked with a strong Scots accent. I agreed it was and asked where we were bound. He told me that we were going to Port Said, Port Tewfik, Hong Kong, Shanghai, Bombay and then home again—about a three months' trip and there were bound to be changes to the itinerary. Sailing next Saturday, we carried troops in the troop decks and officers and their wives in the passenger accommodation. Warrant officers and their wives went second-class in the poop. Mr Nixon explained that he was the second officer. 'You are going to have to find your own level and friends, laddie', he continued. 'The four deck officers are all holders of masters' licences and we all live in the same accommodation behind the bridge, where no one can go except on business. There are a couple of engineers making their first trip that you ought to get to know; they live in the alleyway by your cabin.' I asked why all the deck officers were so highly qualified. It was 1929 and the depression had really hit shipping. 'Ellerman City Line has been laying up passenger ships and the Hall & Bucknell side of the combine that operates the cargo boats are having a struggle to find any cargoes at all. You haven't picked a very good time to start your seagoing carrier. The rivers of this country will be full of laid-up ships in a year's time.' A true prophecy—but I was more interested in how a trooper operated.

Mr Nixon explained that the service passengers all came under the OC troops, while the civilian crew came under the captain. An extra deck officer was carried to act as liaison between the two camps, and there were a few service people that stayed in the ship regardless of whom we carried. He said that it usually worked out well, especially with a lascar crew, and that there was not much fraternisation between the Services and the European officers. 'We have jobs to do and there isn't much common ground even if we are carrying naval detachments', he said. He explained that there was nothing for me to do until the senior operator returned from his leave on Friday. I then asked him the question that had been on my mind since I had first heard of the *City of Marseilles*. 'What sort of a chap is the senior operator?' I asked. Mr Nixon swung his chair round and stood up. 'That you must find out for yourself, old son. He is an Irishman called Farrell and don't lend him any money.' With this cryptic advice he strode away across the deserted saloon. With the knowledge that at least somebody didn't like my new boss, I found my way back to my cabin. It was all too new to assimilate and I turned into the lower berth. Bunks weren't the same as beds —the blankets and sheets were folded together and not tucked in—but it didn't matter, I slept like a top until the boy called me for breakfast. 'Tea, Sahib, breakfast in half hour, you wear shore suit?' Even the boy seemed to dislike me wearing my brave new outfit ashore.

I had breakfast with Mr Nixon, who surveyed my shore suit with approval. 'That's better, laddie, you off ashore?' I said I was going to the radio company's office, and later climbed down the gangway and set off across the docks. My only real concern was that I would not be easily recognisable as the second radio officer of HMT *City of Marseilles*. I took a long way to the radio company's office, examining every ship in the docks, rolling their names over my tongue— *Hardwick Grange, Llanstephen Castle, Nurturton*, none of them sounded as well as *City of Marseilles*. I entered the office with a little more confidence this time and found that the men sitting round had been replaced by another very similar collection, but my friend Paddy was missing. The staff clerk eyed me with irritation. 'Why didn't you report back here after you had signed on?' he demanded. 'No one said anything about it', I replied. He turned away. 'Just as long as you're there on sailing day, I couldn't care less.'

As I sat down on one of the benches, I was joined by a well dressed man who didn't seem to fit in with the rest of the waiting ones, even to my uneducated mind. He told me that he was the representative of the Association of Wireless and Cable Telegraphists for the area, and spent the next five minutes telling me where my duty lay. This organisation eventually became the Radio Officers' Union or the ROU. He explained that the big problem about being the representative of a seagoing union was collecting the subscriptions, and it would simplify things if I would make the Association an allotment from my salary that would then be paid every month. This I did, with the unwilling co-operation of the staff clerk.

The next forty-eight hours went in a daze. Mr Nixon was replaced as duty officer by a long dour Scotchman who turned out to be the chief officer. We had our meals together in absolute silence.

I was sitting in the radio room on the Thursday morning when the door opened and in walked the first operator. He was short and stout with black curly hair, and as Irish as my first friend Paddy. Farrell was probably forty years old, with a growing family in a tiny village in the south of Ireland which seemed to make such demands on his salary that his temper was permanently sour and his pockets permanently empty. Looking back, I suppose that the business of taking an absolutely green junior away each trip was enough to sour any man. He discussed the job for a time, explaining that with two men the watches were divided into six hours and two hours, and that I would have to do the six hours at night and one two-hour spell in the day. He showed me the switches to close to operate the receiver, borrowed my last £2 and suggested I spent the rest of the day listening in on 600m to see what I made of it. We met again the next morning at breakfast.

The next day the ship filled up with troops, seemingly thousands of them, and the first problem became apparent: the deck around the radio room was for other ranks, and for the rest of the voyage it was packed with troops during all the hours of daylight. The enclosure outside my cabin turned out to be the troops' lavatories—galvanised troughs along which was pumped a steady flow of salt water.

At midday on Saturday, two tugs came alongside, the haze over the top of the funnel thickened into a rolling black cloud, and a feather of steam spouted from the brass whistle on the funnel, followed by the boom from the whistle, a sound that was to be associated in my mind with sailing days as long as I stayed at sea. The rails were jammed with troops trying to find somewhere to watch the sailing. Over the heads of the soldiers I was aware that the cranes on the dockside were moving back along the dock walls. His Majesty's Transport *City of Marseilles* was leaving Southampton for Shanghai.

Farrell decreed that I should take the first two hours, and, as the ship steamed down the Solent, I began my first watch at sea. I could read morse or thought I could, but it seemed that every ship's radio operator was pounding on his key that afternoon; this was before the days of continuous wave transmitters and the noise created by various types of spark transmitter was incredible; but with the aid of a book on call signs I attempted to unravel the chaos. One particularly noisy spark became Land's End and a high pitched whine sounding like E R E R E A eventually became F F U, the French station at Ushant. Periodically G L D would call C Q 'all ships', followed by a list of four-letter ships' call signs. I copied one of these down and then busied myself to see what ships they were. One of them was G C P Y which, when I looked it up, was the *City of Marseilles*. For five minutes I sat in blind panic, afraid to answer. Farrell came in a few minutes later, but he didn't seem to worry. 'I'll get it later', he promised and vanished again. I glanced up at the clock on the bulkhead and suddenly had the most horrible feeling that the whole bulkhead had moved towards me. I glanced away and was then conscious that it again leaned towards me. Gradually I lost interest in the morse pouring into my ears. I was beginning to feel distinctly giddy.

Farrell poked his head in the door. 'Come and get your dinner', he said. I climbed over the high sill of the radio room, stepped unsteadily round the groups of soldiers squatting all over the deck, and entered the long alleyway that led forward to the saloon. The deck was unsteady now; as I put my foot down, it came up to meet me and I stumbled. I sat down in the fixed chair at the usual table. Trying hard to appear normal, I concentrated on the menu, and found that the only easy thing to read was roast lamb. The galley was not yet fully organised and I waited an agonising ten minutes for my order to appear. When it arrived, it was cold and a margin of congealed white fat had formed round the edge of the plate. I remember stumbling down that long alleyway to the afterdeck where the radio cabin was. For a minute the fresh air seemed to revive me, but then it came. Pushing aside soldiers who were peering over the rails for their last glimpse of England, I was violently sick over the side. Temporarily relieved, I found my way down to the cabin and flung myself on the settee.

Farrell aroused me some time later, claiming it was time to start my six-hour stint. I don't know how long I stayed up in that radio room between trips to the rail, but suddenly the feeling came over me that I wasn't doing any good at this wireless business at all, and that it would be better to die; and for fourteen days it was thought that I might. The ship's doctor afterwards told me that it was the most prolonged bout of seasickness that he had seen, and it was decided that I was to be put ashore in Port Said. I can remember little about it except odd pictures of the sea periodically washing over the glass porthole, and an elderly woman feeding me brandy and milk. Then one morning I woke up cured. I felt incredibly weak and my uniform hung on me like a sack, but my mind was clear and I no longer felt sick.

My progress back to the wireless room was slow, but I think Farrell was as pleased to see me as he could be pleased about anything, and promptly borrowed my spare black tie. At lunchtime I navigated that long alleyway again, but this time I was ravenously hungry. My old acquaintance, Mr Nixon, was in his usual place, but the other faces at the table were new. I found that my illness had gained me some slight recognition and they all had a kind word to say; even the ship's doctor walked across from his table and made a joke at my ravenous appetite. 'Not too much, laddie', he laughed, 'I know you have fourteen days to make up, but don't try and do it in one meal.' He then suggested to Farrell that I started watchkeeping when we left Port Said. I retired to my bunk after lunch and, when the boy arrived with the afternoon tea, the ship was moored to the dolphins at Port Said. I was too frail to go ashore, but, when we left at about 6.0pm, I started my six-hour watch. 'Tell Alex we have left', said Farrell, 'and then try and copy the Press from Rugby at twenty hundred.' Slowly I pulled over the starter motor handle to the mounting whine of the generator; the handle held and I pushed over the Send/Receive switch. I slowly keyed S U H de G A C P Y, and Alexandria replied immediately. 'City of Marseilles leaving Port Said for Port Tewfik', I sent, and received an 'OK'. Another milestone had been passed.

I enjoyed my first six-hour watch—the ship was sailing quietly down the Suez Canal in brilliant moonlight, the air waves were quiet and there was nothing for me to do but sit on the high doorstep of the radio cabin and admire the night. A few army detachments were picked up at Port Tewfik, and after an hour at anchor we steamed out into the Red Sea—next stop Hong Kong.

I had no help from Farrell at all, but gradually by tria and error I began to get the hang of the job. I sometimes think that finding one's own way is the most satisfactory method of learning. My relations with Farrell were hard to define. I must have been incredibly naive, and there could not have been any common ground upon which to build up any sort of companionship. He had spent years at sea on dozens of tramp steamers, and knew even less of shore life than I did. His knowledge of the sea, ships and the world's seaways was comprehensive: he had, for instance, been two years on the China coast, three years on the Chilean coast, and two years on the Indian coast. In those days there were three classes of ship, each with different salaries for the radio operator—Class I, a passenger ship with a total complement of over 100; Class II, over fifty and below 100; and the Class III ship, which made up the bulk of shipping, with a complement of less than fifty. The ladder from Class III to Class I was a long and arduous climb that had nothing to do with ability; a promotion to a higher class was usually a matter of how well your face fitted with that omnipotent arbitrator of destinies, the staff clerk, and if you had enough years in the radio company to prevent people from being too jealous.

The *City of Marseilles* was Farrell's first Class I ship, but he was far from happy about it, for she was laying up after this voyage and he knew that he would have to join the long queue of senior men waiting for Class I ships again. The problem of supporting his family and himself on a small salary also weighed heavily on his mind. The rest of the deck officers had Farrell's problems to a greater or lesser degree. The great slump was just beginning and most companies were being forced to lay up their ships and discharge their crews. To keep some of the officers in employment, they were putting them in positions sometimes two grades down: the second and third officers had both been reduced from chief officers, but were glad to get positions at all.

I was thrown on to the engine-room staff to find companionship. There were eight engineers on board and an electrician. The seventh and eighth engineers were first trippers, just out of their apprenticeships, and the electrician was also a first tripper, though a married man with two children. The latter's sister had married a radio operator, and after I had recovered from my bout of seasickness he made a point of seeking me out. Soon we got to know each other and would spend our off-watch periods sitting and chatting in each other's cabins. There was no spare deck to sit on, for they were black with troops all day long and some of the nights, too, in the hot weather.

Troopers are odd types of ship to sail in. They are terribly noisy and crowded; once on board a ship, a soldier stamps everywhere. If he is on guard at a ladder, he periodically smashes the butt of his rifle on the deck. His deck games, drills, etc, on the *City of Marseilles* were all accompanied by a frenzied bellowing, though the crowning noise came one afternoon when the fife and drum band had a practice session on the hatch outside the radio room. The din was so indescribable that in desperation I appealed to Farrell, and, as it was disturbing his afternoon sleep, he appealed to the troop officer and at least we got that racket stopped.

The only type of gambling allowed the troops officially was a game called housey-housey (just like bingo). Through all the hours of daylight this interminable game continued on the deck surrounding the radio cabin. I can remember the chanting of Kelly's eye, legs eleven and clickety-click, but in the end I could keep a radio watch through it all, for when you grew used to it, you did not consciously listen at all, but the call sign of your own ship was equivalent to someone calling your name.

The Red Sea was terribly hot, but there was a scoop that could be pushed through the open porthole to catch a steady stream of air caused by the passage of the ship. We passed Aden—just a loom of light in the night sky—and then sailed out into the Indian Ocean. The next day the steady thump of engines was suddenly stilled in the middle of the afternoon watch—we had come on a dhow flying a distress flag and had stopped to investigate. All hands hung over the rails watching as a dugout canoe left the dhow's side and paddled alongside the ship. The two men in the dugout explained in pantomime that they were starving and out of water. They were the blackest men I had ever seen, seeming to be burnt almost blue by the blazing sun. Petrol tins of water were lowered to them, and rice and bread, until the dugout was almost awash. The dhow manoeuvred nearer the ship and then, as the *City of Marseilles* was eased very gently ahead, slid neatly alongside the dugout and scooped it up. Soon the dhow was a tiny white blob against the glittering sea.

At dinner that night, I, greatly daring, asked the Scots chief officer, who was alone at the table when I sat down, what had really been wrong. 'It's an old trick, laddie', he explained in his strong Scots accent. 'Most of those dhows do a trip a year from the Persian Gulf to the East Coast of Africa and back again. That one was on her way back to the Persian Gulf with a cargo of mangrove poles. She could have been weeks on the way from some creek in East Africa where they chopped those poles, and her water supplies could well have been infected when they sailed. They live just on the edge of starvation and sleep on the cargo. Must be a hell of a life. The problem is that they always aim for the steamer tracks coming out of the Red Sea and stop us for food and water whether they are short or not.' Mr Nixon had joined us and broke in: 'I remember once being stopped by a schooner in the Bristol Channel that was out of food. When asked how many days out of Swansea they were, the Welsh skipper shouted "Two days tomorrow, man" '.

The next incident of interest was a radio message from Aden instructing the captain to proceed to Colombo. The captain was a great character. Apparently there were two captains with the same surname in the company; to distinguish them one was called 'Gentleman' Booth and the other 'Bastard' Booth—and we had the latter. He was a short powerful man with close-trimmed grey hair and a red apoplectic face that always seemed on the point of bursting into flame. I only spoke to him once and that could hardly be called a conversation. In Shanghai one morning I noticed that the ship was bedecked with flags—the second officer had had all the signal flags washed and they had been hung up to dry. I asked him why the flags were up and he turned and eyed me with concern. 'Laddie, it's the captain's birthday; haven't you wished him "happy returns" yet?' I claimed that no one had told me. 'That's Farrell's job, not mine', he answered. 'Best go along about 10 o'clock and do it.' At 10 sharp I climbed to that holy of holies, the bridge—the Captain's cabin was behind the bridge—and tapped timidly on the louvred panel of the door. There was a muffled snarling noise and then silence. I waited, then there was a roaring. I couldn't distinguish the words, so I pushed open the door and found Bastard Booth in his pyjama trousers shaving. The bottom half of his face was covered with lather, and when he saw me the top half turned purple. I quickly wished him 'Many happy returns of the day'.

For ten seconds he gazed at me in utter disbelief, then he mumbled and pointed to the settee. I sat and waited. The air was electric, and I could feel my flesh crawl while he vanished into his bedroom and eventually came back dressed in his uniform, less his white jacket. He said: 'Now what the hell's all this about? "Happy returns" be damned. Who in hell said it was my bloody birthday?' 'Well Sir, you see I noticed that all the flags were up and when I made some enquiries I found that it was to celebrate your birthday.' 'And which one of the officers and bloody gentlemen told you that?' he asked. The trap was now obvious and I had to get out without further discussion. 'Well Sir, nobody exactly; you see, Sir, it just seemed the right thing to do.'

'You don't want to tell me?'

'No, Sir', I replied.

'Might as well assume it is my birthday, I suppose', and he promptly poured me out a half glass of whisky. 'Straight doon, laddie', he said, 'and then straight doon off my deck.' I swallowed the burning spirit—it tasted like hell, and I can only liken it to swallowing a length of red hot chain. With my eyes blurred with tears from the burning, I walked down to my cabin and swallowed at least a gallon of water. I have always regretted that I was not able to sustain my initial dislike of Scotch whisky.

Colombo appeared out of the sea one glorious tropical morning just as my watch was finishing. It was my first foreign port in the real sense of the word. The *City of Marseilles* tied up to a mooring buoy in the middle of Colombo harbour early in the morning. Again she was only discharging and loading small detachments of troops before carrying on to Hong Kong, where the majority of our passengers were destined. I was very keen on a short run ashore, but my engineering friends were asleep and everyone else was desperately busy preparing for a midday departure, so I had to content myself with the view from the rails. At midday the boom of the steam whistle presaged that Colombo was going to join the list of places we had visited but where my acquaintance with the shore was a view of a dock wall.

I soon settled down to my six-hour night and two-hour day watches again while we steamed across the Indian Ocean to the Straits of Malacca. The weather was still and hot, and my only problem was getting an unbroken sleep in the morning, for the army continued to make as much noise as ever. Singapore was just a blaze of light in the night sky, and then we turned north again for our first real stop of the voyage—Hong Kong. Farrell now told me that the radio company had an office in Hong Kong and that quite a number of radio men were based there for duty on the China coast. If one of them had completed his two years' 'China coast' duty, I could well replace him and he would return home in the ship. If this was supposed to put me off, he was wrong. As I hadn't come to sea for the noise and congestion of a trooper, two years on the China coast presented no problems.

On the morning of the ninth day out from Colombo, the Lyee Moon Pass into Hong Kong came up out of the mist and we steamed into the harbour. What a sight for a first tripper! High mountains, indistinct in the heat haze all round, and the surface of the harbour chock full of ships—ferries from the mainland, the White Empresses of the Canadian Pacific line, sidewheel paddlers from the Chinese rivers, cargo boats of every nationality in all states of loading and discharge, and the whole picture interwoven with the movements of junks and sampans. The big stately junks with their matting sails hardly seemed to move at all, but the sampans scuttled around like water bugs. The ship was berthed in Kowloon and Farrell insisted on my going ashore with him to report at the office. If he got a junior man in Hong Kong, he was bound to be of more use to him than I was. We crossed to the mainland and found the company's office. They had no need of a junior of my tender experience, so I had the honour of treating Mr Farrell to a few drinks, the money for which he lent me out of the radio cashbox. I thought perhaps it would be offset against what he owed me. In the afternoon, the seventh engineer and I explored Kowloon, and were back on board for dinner.

My first and most lasting impression of Hong Kong was of the noise of the streets, everyone calling, talking, shouting or quarrelling to a background of continuous clatter from wooden sandals. We sailed early in the morning and four mornings later I watched our arrival at Shanghai. It was very different from Hong Kong, the ship seeming to creep along on a muddy flood for hours while the low-lying banks drew slowly closer. In those days Shanghai was a series of concessions—the French Concession, the British Concession and so on—each one fronting the River Yangtze, and each concession took on the appearance and way of life of the nation that sponsored it. The nightclubs and bars of Shanghai were filled with Russian refugees who had fled to China during the Revolution. They came mostly from the middle classes and some of them had a great battle simply to exist in that great sprawling Chinese city. Poverty was rife among the millions of Chinese themselves, and life was cheap. The ship was moored to buoys and a barge was moored alongside to carry out some engine-room repairs. I remember seeing what appeared to be a woman and a child, who had obviously drowned, stuck on one of the barge's fenders; a coolie from the barge just pushed the bodies free from the fender and they were swirled away in the mud-coloured flood of the Yangtze.

The junior engineers and I made two expeditions ashore, but they were only partly successful. We were dogged by howling mobs of rickshaw coolies until, in sheer defence, we took two of them. They trotted into the first whorehouse compound in the French Concession and demanded a huge sum. The haggling was complicated by language problems, and Russian prostitutes then further complicated matters by running off with the engineers' caps into their house. One particularly hideous Russian prostitute professed to take a fancy to me and further involved my negotiations with the rickshaw boy by offering me the use of her young sister for one dollar Mex—a large silver Maria Theresa dollar marked with indelible ink of some sort. I think this marking was to prove its authenticity, for the whole monetary system was clogged with counterfeit money. There were even counter-

31

feit cash, and that was a tiny copper coin of infinitesimal value with a hole in the middle; I believe a foot long string of them was worth 6d. We extricated ourselves forcibly from the compound and found our way to the Bund or river front, still pursued by the howling mob of rickshaw boys. In desperation we climbed into the two rickshaws again and headed back to the ship. At the foot of the gangway the haggling broke out once more, but this time an ally turned up—a large bearded Sikh policeman strolled over. 'How long, Sahib, you have this boy?' We explained for about half an hour. 'Give me half dollar for each boy. I settle.' This we did, and climbed up the gangway to an absolute torrent of abuse from the rickshaw boys. Hardly the impassive orientals I had read about in books!

Mr Nixon was amused next morning at breakfast. 'I suggest you young men aim to go to the Seamen's Mission on the Bund in the British Concession the next time you go ashore. Those Russian prostitutes are poxed up to the eyebrows in the French Concession and you don't want a dose of clap on your first trip.' We didn't exactly follow his advice, but confined our shoregoing to the hours of daylight.

Now we loaded up again with a mixture of contingents from all the Services—mostly sailors and soldiers who had been in China for years. One Army sergeant, complete with Chinese wife and two half-caste children, had been there seven years, and was full of questions about 'home'. He would sit on the step of the radio cabin and question me for hours. He obviously had a big readjustment to face, particularly as he had been on a detachment inland at Ichang, and not in a big city like Shanghai.

After about a week we sailed south to Hong Kong, where we were scheduled to embark a battalion that had been away from England for five years. My sergeant friend told me that some of the soldiers had been with the battalion all the time, though a percentage of both men and officers had been rotated home. The trip to Hong Kong was uneventful, but the embarkation of the regiment was far from so. It started the morning after we had docked and it was a complete shambles. The army officers and MPs did their best, but the men had been abroad too long and they were now going home. Drunk, fighting, singing and trying to drag their Chinese girl friends along, they were eventually taken on board and below decks, and we sailed for Bombay. Farrell now warned me that I would be very lucky to get away from Bombay without being posted to the Indian coast.

C

CHAPTER THREE

Pilgrims to Jeddah

T H E radio company's Bombay office had numerous two-man
ships on its books, and there was bound to be someone waiting to go home. The ship berthed at Ballard Pier in Bombay
early one morning, and, within an hour, Farrell called me to
the radio cabin. 'They want you to report to the office at
once', he said. 'I'll come along and show you the way. I know
the super here very well.' The office was just outside the dock
gates, a replica of the Southampton office; except that the
staff clerk was now a Parsee, and a voluble friendly little man
he turned out to be. As long as you called him 'Mister', he
would do anything for you. 'You have been appointed third
man on a Hadji ship', he told me in his singsong English. He
flicked over my paybook. 'We pay you in rupees now. You go
back to City boat, pay your bill and then come back here. I
send messenger to show you shipping office to sign off.' I
walked back to the ship and asked the boy for my bill, for in
ships you just signed a chit for cigarettes and drinks and then
at the end of the voyage settled what you owed. I now found
the weakness of the system. It was easy to sign and difficult to
pay, and it took almost every rupee of the slender bundle that
the Parsee staff clerk had given me to clear my debt. The
ship's boy loaded my baggage in an open carriage or ghaïri,
accepted a few more rupees and I set off back to the office.
The clerk clucked at my parsimonious state. 'I make you 20
rupees advance', he smiled, and presented me with a form to

sign on for the steam vessel *Sultania*. Farrell came out of the superintendent's office just as I was leaving, but he didn't want to know me. He had my replacement with him, a man of almost his own age, so I said goodbye to my money, my spare black tie and HMT *City of Marseilles*.

She sailed back to England and was replaced in the trooping fleet by the Bibby liner *Lancashire*. The *City of Marseilles* had been built by Palmer's Shipbuilding Company at Hebburn-on-Tyne in 1913 for the Hall line of Liverpool, which transferred her to the Ellerman City Line management in 1919. She was to return to trooping in the early part of World War II, sustain mine damage off the Tay in January 1940, and eventually be wrecked off the coast of Ceylon in January 1943.

Back at the radio company's office the Parsee staff clerk met me at the door. 'You are most lucky man', he said in the odd voice that the Indian develops when he uses English as his second language. 'Chief operator from the *Sultania* has come up to the office and I have asked him to wait for you.' I found Cara Jones a different character from Master Farrell. He was about twenty-five years old, dressed in khaki shorts and shirt, with a khaki Bombay bowler balanced on the back of his head. He was a friendly soul and, although 100 per cent Wesh, spoke English without the trace of an accent. He told me later that he came from the 'Little England beyond Wales' and had been born in Neyland, Pembrokeshire. I explained my movements and he said: 'Don't worry, old son, we'll get the staff clerk to tell the gharri to take your gear down to the ship, where the butler will pay him for the journey. You and I will go and have a beer in the 'Alexander' after we've got you signed off and on, and when we are ready we'll go down to the ship in a tram.'

This was arranged and we later walked round to the 'Alexander'; I was really feeling the heat in my English clothes and that beer tasted good. Cara had been on the Indian coast for two years and was to become a real friend. 'First thing is to get you some tropical kit. It's as hot as hell on the *Sultania*;

no one wears uniform, just shorts and shirt and sandals. There is a tailor outside the dock gate that sells ready made; we'll call on him on the way back to the ship. He'll also fix you up with a topee.' This was the local name for the lightweight cork hat that everybody wore during the day. I pointed out that the rupee situation might become acute, but he only smiled. 'He would be put out if you paid him before the end of the month; what guarantee would he have that you would go back to him for anything else you wanted?'

Cara then told me about my new ship. The *Sultania* was an old German vessel of about 4,000 tons that had been converted to carry pilgrims from Bombay and Karachi to Jeddah, the port for Mecca, in the Red Sea. She was twenty-two years old and steamed along at 9 knots, driven by an ancient triple expansion steam engine that might have been used to move Noah's ark along. Because she carried thousands of passengers, more than many of the liners, she had three radio men—Cara, a chap called Groves, and now me. The crew were very mixed but quite friendly. At the moment she was laid up in an out-of-the-way corner of the docks waiting for the next Hadji season to start in about six weeks' time. I bombarded Cara with questions, which he answered patiently. When I mentioned the radio equipment, he smiled 'Don't worry about that. The gear is so old, it's laughable. It actually has a crystal receiver and one of the first spark transmitters ever built. It makes so much bloody noise that you can hear it all over the ship. The so-called silence cabinet is alongside the Old Man's bunk, and a sure way of bringing down hell and damnation on your head is to blast it off about half an hour after he has turned in. Groves and you have a two-berth cabin and I have one on my own', he continued. 'Don't worry about accommodation, it's so damned hot we all live out on deck and sleep on camp beds.' Cara finished his beer. 'Let's catch the tram down to the dock gate, see the tailor and we can be aboard for "tiffin".' Tiffin turned out to be lunch.

Cara and I climbed aboard a tram outside the 'Alexander' and sat down on the wooden seats. The tram was crowded with Indians in their shirts and dhotis and little round hats. They swarmed all over the tram like ants, they clung by the dozen to the steps, they all shouted at the top of their voices and chewed the bright red betel nut. I thought Hong Kong was noisy but Bombay had it beaten by a mile. Slowly the tram clanged its noisy way down the long dock road. The tracks were covered with oxen drawing loud-squeaking carts, holy cows with a hump on their backs and thousands of people walking and cycling. Cara sat quietly beside me and smoked; he had seen this teeming scene many times before and it was too noisy to talk.

At the time I thought it something of a come-down for the British Raj, but I was soon to find that my 90 odd rupees a month did not allow many taxis from the ship to the office. It was barely enough to live on, since most of us had commitments at home to pay the money spent in financing us during the period of getting our tickets. At last the long ride was over, and Cara walked towards a row of open-fronted shops with matting roofs to shade them from the sun. The shop he entered looked like a black cave, but when my vision had adjusted itself from the sunlight to the gloom I could see that about a dozen men were sitting cross-legged before hand-driven Singer sewing machines, stitching industriously. We were met at the entrance by Mr Bannerjee himself, identifiable from his workers only by his round white hat and flow of singsong English.

'Bannerjee, you robbing bastard, I bring you new No 3 man', said Cara.

'Jones, sahib, you speak badly of Bannerjee to new No 3—"robbing bastard" no good.' He shook me warmly by the hand. 'Me good tailor, very quick, very cheap, money come bye and bye, Bannerjee he no worry.' I was to find later that this was absolutely true. From the staff clerk Bannerjee knew everyone's credit rating down to the last anna, and woe betide anyone who thought he would slip away without paying Bannerjee's bill; he knew before you did what ship you were going home on. In short order he produced two pairs of shorts, and two khaki shirts that were 'brand new, No 3 sahib. Built for No 3 of *Viceroy of India*, very special passenger ship man, he very unlucky No 3, he leave just before shirts were ready'. 'Ducked you, eh? Bannerjee', said Cara. 'No Jones, Sahib, good No 3 Viceroy man, one day he come back to pay Bannerjee.' Cara turned to me: 'Bloody right he will; if he turns up anywhere on the Indian Coast, they'll find out, they're uncanny about finding English debtors. I heard once of a steward in a mailboat who bilked a tailor and then went home and joined the army. Some years later he was posted to India in the *Neuralia*; as she warped into Ballard Pier, the tailor was waiting to greet him'. Cara looked at his watch. 'We'd better push on, fairish walk to the ship; this lot'll be aboard before we are', he said.

We found the *Sultania* tied up to the quay in a completely deserted dock. She was of 4,379 tons gross, with black-painted hull, stone-coloured deck houses, and a tall thin funnel that betrayed her age. That funnel was the only striking thing about her: it was painted a dull yellow and carried a broad white band liberally bedecked with quarter moons and stars painted in bright blue. She had been built as the *Kerman* in 1907, and was later called the *Furth*, before being bought by the Persian Gulf Steam Navigation Company of Bombay. Cara and I climbed the wooden gangway and I followed him along a narrow alleyway in the midship house into an old-fashioned panelled saloon. There were two other officers in for tiffin—the second mate and the second radio man, Groves. He was an eager young man of twenty who was determined to rise above the lowly position in which he now found himself. He spent most of his days and nights ashore with his friends and we saw very little of him. He appeared to haunt the Flying Angel mission to seamen, where he had wormed his way into the 'shore wallah' fraternity that visited the mission to entertain the sailors ashore. English deckhands were remarkably scarce in Bombay, since all coastal cargo was carried by ships with lascar crews and British officers, and all the mailboats had lascar crews. The only ships with English crews were the odd tramps that wandered in with a bulk cargo. Groves took full advantage of this and accepted every invitation he had to go ashore. He despised Cara and me for staying aboard an old Indian-owned ship in a deserted dock at the end of the tramline. Perhaps he was right, but after going out with him for an evening I was completely disillusioned with his glamorous 'shore wallah' friends.

I was to learn that in those days the British in India were divided by a caste system just as rigid as that which applied to the natives. At the top of the social strata were the sahibs who worked in every branch of industry, on the next level were the officers on ships operating along the Indian coast and on the lowest level were the British soldiers on postings in India. The second mate of the *Sultania*, Mr Baugh, was a member of yet another strata of Indian society—a half-caste or a Chee Chee, as they were generally called.

During the six weeks we waited in that deserted dock for the Hadji season to begin, Cara and I came to know Mr Baugh very well. He spent most of the day snarling around the ship, and then departed each evening after supper to spend the night at home. On the third day during lunch he asked me what religion I was. I felt Cara kick my leg, but the warning passed unheeded and I replied that I was an agnostic; I had not been baptised, for my parents had felt that I should be allowed to reach the age of twenty-one before deciding on my particular brand of religion, if any. Mr Baugh's face turned almost grey with rage. For an hour he ranted about sitting down with heathens, and the mildest thing he promised me was that I would be struck down on the deck as a blasphemer. He would not sail with me; as soon as the captain joined he would have me signed off the ship... Suddenly the placid Cara had had enough, and turned on Baugh: 'That's enough, you asked No 3 his religion and he told you. What he is is not your business, so drop it'. Baugh was amazed. 'You Welsh swine, I am the second officer and in the absence of the captain I insist that this man leave the saloon. This is a God-fearing ship.' Cara had heard more than enough. 'Listen, you half black bastard son of a bloody swoddy, we eat in this saloon; you can eat in hell'. Baugh turned even greyer and I remember noticing the sweat drip from his chin on to his white shirt. He had been told the thing that could hurt him most—that he wasn't white. He took his meals ashore from then on until we sailed, and he never spoke to any of us again.

Two days later the captain turned up on board. Captain Merryleas was a Scot in his early sixties who had been thirty years on Indian coast ships and spoke the Hindustani language almost as well as his own. He was a pleasant man but incredibly remote. He would chat to Cara and me for hours and yet neither of us could say that we were any closer to him as the weeks went by. He was unmarried, and never spoke of any family back in Scotland or of friends ashore in India. When I left the *Sultania*, Captain Merryleas passed out of my life for ever. I was to return to the Indian coast in later years but I could find no one who knew where he had gone. When the *Sultania* was eventually sold in Rangoon, he just vanished ashore.

Some days after his return, the captain called me up to his cabin on the lower bridge. 'I hear you have been having some trouble with the second mate, young Sparks. You appear to have some conflicting views and he wants you moved.' 'That's the trouble, Sir, I haven't any views at all and it made him mad.' The Captain smiled his remote smile. 'He is a very bigoted man, I'm afraid—comes from a devout Roman Catholic family, his wife is half Portuguese and is a rabid Catholic. I think some of this business of getting you off the ship stems from her.' He smiled again. 'I think the general idea is that fire could fall from heaven on your head and they don't want it to happen when he is on the *Sultania* with you. I have no intention of signing you off, but take this as a warning; don't argue about religion in a ship, there's no room to get away.'

The first officer was an Indian. He took all his meals in his room, as did the captain, and spoke only to the crew in Hindustani; he spoke good English but preferred not to do so.

The chief and second engineers were from Mauritius but had both been years on Indian coast ships and were completely bilingual; they lived entirely in the engineers' mess room. I soon became familiar with the old ship; both the decks and the 'tween decks were sheeted with concrete, because the pilgrims carried and cooked their own food on the trip to Jeddah and back. Beside the tiny cabin that Groves and I were supposed to share was another one for two native doctors who would join the ship with the pilgrims. There was also another tiny cabin for two ships' clerks, called 'crannys'. The ship supplied the pilgrims with water, but nothing else. The cabins were tiny, just two bunks with straw mattresses and a strange device, often found in old ships, called a compactum. It had a water tank in the top compartment, and a bowl and tap in the second, which you emptied into a tank in the bottom compartment by closing it up.

Cara explained that none of the accommodation was habitable when the pilgrims were on board, and that the crannys let all the cabins and the deck outside them, even the saloon and the deck outside the radio cabin. The captain retained his cabin and deck, but the rest of us migrated to the big open flying bridge, where we slept on camp beds and had our meals under a double awning. He explained that it was the only way to live on a pilgrim ship: the noise and the smell made the main decks uninhabitable, and, anyway, the share of the renting fees added up to quite a few rupees—a welcome addition to our minute monthly salaries. I was quite happy to accept this arrangement, but the No 2, Groves, had other views. He wanted to hang on to the tiny cabin that was Cara's by right, but he gave it up and joined us on the bridge two days after the pilgrims joined; four men had moved in and had slept on the cabin floor the first night out, and refused to move.

The captain said the ship was actually owned by a Bengali named Mehta. He just navigated the ship between the ports, while the passengers and their fares were a matter for the native crannys or pursers, call them what you will. The man in charge of this side of the operation was Mr Mehta's brother-in-law. The Indian doctors were put aboard by the Government and paid by it.

On the day before sailing, we all moved up to our new quarters at the back of the open bridge, and, before full light the peace of that silent old ship in her deserted dock was completely shattered. The pilgrims poured down to the dockside in their thousands, using everything on wheels and feet they could find to carry their goods, their food, their cooking pots, their bedclothes. As I watched them filing up the gangway and past the two watchful native clerks at the head of it, I was struck by their age and apparent poverty. Captain Merryleas came and leant over the rail alongside me and I remarked on this. 'We only get the poor pilgrims that can't afford to travel on the better class pilgrim ships', he replied. 'It's a great sign of their faith. These people have worked and saved all their lives to make this trip to Mecca before they die. The tragedy is that many will die before they get to Mecca and even more will die before they see Bombay again. Some of the older ones are just satisfied that they have lived long enough to have made the pilgrimage, and their will to continue living will be gone on the voyage home.' 'How many of them are there, Sir?' I asked the captain. He eyed me quizzically. 'Sparks, I know how many I am licensed to carry but how many we actually finish up with only the clerks know, and they would never tell. Actually, each person is allocated a certain amount of space, but ...', he shrugged his shoulders, 'backsheesh performs all sorts of miracles in this country. I have been on these ships for years. We even had the Government aboard once to count them to see if we were exceeding our quota. It didn't work; the pilgrims had paid their savings to go to Mecca and they saw the count as a Government fiddle to stop them making the trip. They shifted, moved about, changed places—it was impossible to count them.' The Captain walked forward, with me glued to his side. 'It's not a high-class trade, Sparks', he said. 'We don't get the best officers and we operate out of the monsoon

42

season to minimise the risks; but the thought of a collision, a fire, or even a heavy blow, with this cargo, in an old ship like this, haunts me.' That was the only time that I saw Captain Merryleas display any sort of emotion.

All day long the unending string of pilgrims straggled aboard. The derricks had been lowered and an awning stretched over the open hatches, and in the late afternoon I went down on to the main deck to see how they were settling down. The heat and noise were indescribable. The pilgrims were all in a state of near hysteria, which mounted steadily as the sailing time of 6 o'clock approached. There seemed to be as many people on the wharf as on board the ship, and, as the last rope dropped into the dock from the bow, a low wail started up; the booming of the steam whistle acted as a trigger and the wail grew into an indescribable howl. I felt the hair rising on the back of my neck; it was my first experience of mob hysteria and it wasn't pleasant.

With a tug ahead and astern, the *Sultania* was slowly nudged away from the dock wall and into the lock, and by 6.30 we were steaming slowly along the line of ships anchored in the stream; by evening we were plugging slowly out to sea on our way to the port of Jeddah. It was flat calm and hot. Our open-air life began with dinner served on a table at the back of the bridge behind a canvas screen. The butler, or chief steward, as he would be called on an English ship, did his best at first to serve us with European food, but this was largely confined to tinned meats and eggs and chips. Cara and I took to the Indian foods with alacrity, and only Groves remained aloof. If nothing else, the old *Sultania* taught me to like curry and kedgeree. For a few days we used knives and forks, but regrettably we soon found it easier to use our fingers. Baugh viewed us with deep distaste, and confined any remarks he chose to make to Groves. He sneered openly about our 'going native'. 'They'll be wearing a dhoti next', he commented once to Groves. Cara's slow wrath flashed out. 'At least we haven't married a black bint yet.' Baugh's olive face turned grey with rage, and he leapt to his feet. 'You calling my wife a bint?' he shrilled, but Merryleas had sensed trouble and strolled over from the wing of the bridge. 'That's it, the lot of you. Young Sparks can eat his food with his fingers, so can Cara, but I want no quarrelling on this bridge.' Baugh flounced off.

We all slept on camp beds at the back of the bridge, behind a screen. Groves called me at midnight and I went to the radio room for my first watch. It was a still hot night, the only movement of air resulting from the passage of the ship, which was ambling at a gentle 8 knots, trailing a huge cloud of black smoke that settled over the wake like a thunderstorm. I checked the air waves; all was quiet. Faintly I heard a *Jala* boat tell Colombo that she had left Cochin for Madras. I pulled aside the curtain and listened, and was at once aware of movement. Hundreds of people were sleeping all round me, huddled up on their sleeping mats. There was no talking, no mumbling; I was alone in the midst of a huge crowd, an uncanny feeling. I could see that the light over the radio table was reflected in dozens of dark eyes, and it seemed that half those huddled shapes were not asleep but watching me. What were they thinking about? Were they excited by the thought of accomplishing their life's ambition? Were they frightened at the terrible hardships that lay ahead? Were they grieving for the loved ones left on the dockside in Bombay? I closed the curtain to keep the light from them and settled down at the radio table. The air waves were still quiet, except for the crackling static. Colombo sent out a weather report to all ships—calm sea, light westerly wind—and all was quiet again. The thump, thump, thump of the old reciprocating engine was like a lullaby.

At 4 o'clock Cara relieved me and I went up on to the bridge to my camp bed. The boy woke me up with 'chota hazri'—tea, toast and fruit, with which the day started in the tropics. A bathroom consisting of a wooden grid on the floor, a shelf with a hole for a bucket and a mirror to shave by had been put aside for us at the bottom of the bridge ladder on the maindeck. Here we took it in turn to shower and shave.

Back on the bridge it was hot—really hot. An 8 knot wind from astern just about cancelled the breeze from the ship's passage. The decks were full of cooking pots and people, the smoke and smell going straight up. I stood in the wing of the bridge beside the silent first officer, who smiled at the look of disgust on my face. 'Don't worry, young Sparks', he said in cultured English. 'In a few days you won't smell a thing; the first two days on a Hadji ship are always an eye opener.' His words proved to be true, though I did not get used to the heat, which seemed to get worse.

At her stately 8 knots the old *Sultania* plodded on her way to Jeddah. We passed Aden on my watch at about 2 am, just a blaze of lights on the horizon, and next morning woke up in the Red Sea. I was now to find that the Indian Ocean was cool compared with the Red Sea, and by midday the heat was unbearable. The *Sultania* surged along in the flat calm with a slight following wind, the greasy smoke from the funnel going almost straight up. Even the chattering of the pilgrims had died down—it was too hot even for them to talk. I stood beside the captain at the bridge rail. 'I don't like this, young Sparks', he said. 'They are packed in like sardines down there and this blinding heat has got them all on edge; anything can panic them in this state.'

'What can you do about it, Sir?' I asked.

'I'm going to turn her round and steam her into what little wind there is. We'll lose a bit of time but we may lose a damn sight more if that mob runs amuck.'

On his instruction the secunnie at the helm hauled the big old-fashioned wheel fully over. Slowly we swung round until the smoke from the funnel started to float astern. The brass whistle from the engine room shrilled, and I could hear the disembodied voice of the chief engineer through the pipe as he talked. 'Thank God for that, Skipper, the firemen were absolutely finished; the steam has been falling off all morning. The stokehold's like a firebox itself.'

'Shut her right down and get your men up on deck, Chief', replied the captain. 'I'll just let her jog along into what breeze there is for a couple of hours. Mr Mehta can put up with the delay.' I watched the firemen climb out of the fiddley, their few rags black with sweat, and in minutes we were joined on the bridge by Mr Green, the chief. 'I have been plugging up and down the Red Sea for years', he said in his heavily accented English, 'but I have never seen a morning as hot as this.' The sea was flat calm, the coast of Arabia just visible through the haze, while the sky seemed white with heat. 'Don't like the look of the pilgrims', replied the captain. 'They have gone quiet in the last hour, but we only need one untoward incident and we'll have a panic on our hands.' 'We'll drift along until the heat of the day is over, Chief, say 3 o'clock, and perhaps you can whack up an extra knot or so tonight to make up for lost time', said the captain. He turned to me. 'This will make us a bit late getting into Jeddah, but perhaps it will cool down tomorrow.'

Unfortunately the next day was worse and by midday the heat was even more intense. Then came the spark that triggered off the panic. Most of the old coal-burning steamers sooner or later had fires in their bunkers and the *Sultania* was no exception. These fires, rarely serious, were usually caused by spontaneous combustion, and, unfortunately, a small fire broke out in the cross bunker the next morning. The bunker was covered with hatchboards and a tarpaulin and a number of pilgrims had camped on it. The whole ship seemed to have sunk into a lethargy in the intense heat, but that was suddenly shattered by a gabble of Hindustani which grew to a wild yelling. Within seconds smoke was seeping out of the cross-bunker hatch, and before anything could be done the pilgrims surged to their feet and pressed against the rails. The captain hung on to the whistle lanyard in the hope of, distracting their attention but the boom of the whistle was not heard. I don't know if the first pilgrim fell or jumped, but the rails were now lined with people jumping into the sea.

Captain Merryleas rang an emergency stop on the telegraph, jammed on half helm and the *Sultania* drifted in a slow wide curve, leaving hundreds of screaming pilgrims in the sea behind her. The captain's dilemma was obvious—if he went astern to stop the way, hundreds of the swimmers would be chopped up in the screw. He just let her drift while hundreds of pilgrims continued to jump over the side. I saw some who didn't want to jump but were pushed over and then hung on until they were dislodged. Fortunately the native sailors didn't panic: they flung everything that would float overboard and congregated on the lower bridge, led by the head serang and the chief officer. Cara in the radio room flashed out an SOS, which was immediately acknowledged by a Russian tanker. The head serang lowered his boat into the water, the second mate lowered the second boat from the other side of the lower bridge, and the *Sultania* slowly came to a halt. Suddenly the pilgrims stopped jumping for a reason I could never understand. At one second they were piling over the rails, howling with fear, and then they suddenly stopped and started backing off.

The panic was over. We had about 800 people spread out in the water in a huge half-moon behind us. I played a minor part in the whole episode—I just watched. The boats were manned by our Maldavi sailors, who were more at home in the water than on the ship, and they were picking up swimmers as fast as they could. Then the deeply loaded tanker edged gently into the line of swimmers with cargo nets draped along her sides, which the pilgrims clung to. Two more white lifeboats appeared, moved by men sitting upright on the thwarts and pushing to and fro on handles. They were Flemming boats from a Dutch ship, the *Strait Malacca*, that had arrived on the scene. The Russian tanker had now two motorboats in the water and was collecting our erstwhile passengers at a great rate. More ships were arriving in response to Cara's distress call, and two more motor lifeboats joined in the rescue operation. It was afternoon before the last wet bundle had been hauled aboard the *Sultania*. It took days to sort things out, but a final count showed that we had lost about thirty pilgrims, many of whom had been dead when hauled into the boats. By late afternoon the rescue ships had returned both the living and the dead pilgrims, and the rest of the hot night was spent in committing the dead to the deep.

Two days later we anchored in the harbour at Jeddah, and the process of getting the pilgrims ashore started. The ship's gangway was lowered and a pair of shallow barges were pushed alongside by an ancient tug. On to these the pilgrims scrambled, still carrying their pots and pans. For us the voyage was half over but for them the worst part of their journey, to Mecca, was about to begin. The crew spent the next two days washing and scrubbing out the decks and the holds, while we swung at anchor in the blasting heat. The crannys were the only people allowed ashore. We all still lived on the bridge and the captain kept the peace between Cara and myself and Baugh. One evening he told us of his apprenticeship in sail and about his rise to mate on a fourmasted barque, a fascinating story of a way of life at sea with which none of us were ever to be familiar. I remember his favourite sailing ship was the *Mermerus*. Unlike most old square-rigged sailors, he made no claims that going to sea in sail was the only real way of learning the business. He said it was a hard life made worse by poor food and accommodation, and the conspicuous lack of mechanical devices that would have eased some of the backbreaking manual labour so commonplace on the deck of a sailing ship. Cara asked Baugh if he had served his time in sail; for a few seconds he ignored the question, but becoming aware of the quizzical gaze of the captain he at last replied: 'There were no sailing ships left when I served my time. I went to sea in a turret ship in the Clan Line.' I had never seen a turret ship and he was at once deluged with questions, but he jumped to his feet and strode away. The captain answered for him. 'They were much the same as any other ship except that the huge bulges on each side made the deck very narrow and the accommodation very cramped. The one I was in was pretty old. I remember one of the sailors chipping paint on the flat part of the bulge and his chipping hammer went straight through and fell into the hold. They were built to save Suez Canal dues because this construction gave less tonnage on which these dues were calculated.'

At last the weary wait for the return of our passengers was over and the ancient tug arrived alongside with its string of laden barges. I hung from the bridge cab and watched the pilgrims teeming up the gangway, and the first thing that struck me was how quiet they were compared to the vociferous mob that had piled on to the barges for their journey to the shore. They were still carrying their cooking pots, and I noticed an old man carrying a water tin containing a thin green scum. Being the poorest of the pilgrims, the majority of them had walked to Mecca and back. They showed no particular elation at the realisation of their life's ambition, but seemed indescribably weary, and, once they had been given a water ration, they just curled up on the decks and went to sleep.

It took nearly two days to load up again, for some pilgrims were so far gone that they had to be lifted aboard by the after derrick on a wooden cargo platform. The two Indian doctors were now run off their feet attending to the sick, but at last, with a long whistle, we trundled slowly out to sea. Down the Red Sea past Perim Island we thumped along at 8 knots into the Indian Ocean. The heat was nothing like it had been northbound, but even the fresh sea breezes of the Indian Ocean failed to revive our listless passengers. They seemed to have just tired of living, and, in spite of the continuous efforts of the two doctors, we buried about twenty every night. I was relieved when that gloomy fourteen-day voyage was over and we were warped back into the still-deserted dock in Bombay. The same dense crowd that had seen us off was waiting on the dockside to welcome us home again, but it was much quieter. It almost seemed that the waiting crowds were aware of the panic and our tragic journey home, and were awaiting the actual meeting with their relatives before letting themselves rejoice on their return.

We were just sitting down to dinner that evening when the captain came on to the upper bridge. 'I've some pretty important news', he said quietly. 'The ship has been sold to a company in Rangoon and we have to clean her up and take her round there to be handed over. None of you have jobs after we get to Rangoon.' Baugh's eyes seemed to sink back in his head; for a half-caste with only a second mate's ticket jobs were scarce indeed. The captain showed no emotion at all, and this had obviously happened to him before. 'I'll go along and break the news to the engineers', he said, and swung back down the bridge ladder.

Our sailing from Bombay two days later caused no stir. The old *Sultania* just drifted quietly out into the stream and turned south. The ship seemed gloomy and deserted and, although we still slept on the bridge, we took our meals in the saloon again. Only the three radio men were unaffected by the sale of the ship. Under the terms of the shipping articles we had signed in Bombay all the crew had to be returned to the port of signing on. We three had jobs awaiting us there, but the rest of the crew would then have to find other ships. The majority of the Indian coastal steamers were operated by companies based in the United Kingdom—British India, Asiatic Steam, etc, recruited their officers in the UK for a two- or three-year spell on the coast before being returned home for six months' leave—and finding fresh positions was going to be difficult for the *Sultania's* officers.

Fourteen days after leaving Bombay we picked up the pilot and proceeded up the Irrawaddy to Rangoon. We were tied up to a jetty that seemed to be as crowded as the jetty in Bombay when we had left on our first trip. The crowd turned out to be the uncles, aunts and relatives, near and far, of the new owners. They streamed aboard, and swarmed all over the ship, and once again we retired to the top bridge. There Mehta's representative found us and gave us each an envelope containing a ticket from Rangoon to Calcutta by a British India steamer and second-class rail tickets from Calcutta back to Bombay. We were all to join the British India mail-boat *Aronda* the next day as second-class passengers—quite a change from the half-wild life on the bridge of the old *Sul-*

tania. At the last minute it was decided that the rest of the officers would travel later, so we three radio men travelled alone. As the *Aronda* sped down the Irrawaddy at 16 knots, we saw the last of the old ship, still swarming with people, the new owners no doubt trying to find out what they had bought. I never heard of any of the crew again, and the last I heard of the ship was that she had been seized for debt in Calcutta.

After about two and a half days the *Aronda* churned up to the Calcutta pilot cutter, the *Andrew*, which was anchored off the Sunderbunds. The *Andrew* was a smart clipper-bowed steamer, painted white, and she was the floating home of that exalted individual, the Hughli pilot, who, in those days, was considered the cream of the British Merchant Navy. It was a long and difficult passage through the Sunderbunds to the Hughli River proper and up to Calcutta, and the pilots had to serve a long apprenticeship. They used to join the ship complete with helmsmen, leadsmen, apprentice pilots and servants. Cara pointed out perhaps the worst part of the river passage—the James and Mary Sands. A few weeks previously a British tramp had been driven on to the sands by the current and broke her back, and the next time I went up she had vanished.

While Groves and I organised our baggage through the Customs, Cara went ashore to ring the radio company's local office. He came back with the news that they wanted no part of us. We loaded our baggage into a taxi and set off for Howrah station, where we found that the train left for Bombay at 6.0pm. Fortunately we had a second-class carriage to ourselves. The train journey lasted all that night, all the next day and the next night, and we arrived in Bombay early in the morning. The trip was not very interesting. The train stopped and allowed us to have meals in the various station restaurants, but the country seemed half deserted, though every station was swarming with beggars. Each time the train stopped the windows were immediately filled with the supplicating hands of men, women and children, and that cry that is the real call of the East—'Baksheesh, Sahib'. We all arrived back in the Bombay office of the radio company grimy and tired out, but there was to be no stopover. Cara was immediately signed on an Asiatic steamship and sailed that same afternoon to Madras, Groves left to join the *Arabistan*, another Hadji ship lying out in the Stream, and, as was usual at sea, I never met either of them again.

The little Parsee clerk next turned to me. 'Go and get your lunch; this afternoon I find you ship', he smiled. 'What about a night in the Seamen's Mission?' I replied. 'You find ship for me tomorrow?'

'No, have ship for you now but you can't sign on until this afternoon; very good ship', and beyond that he wouldn't go.

I had lunch in the 'Light of Asia' and returned, now thoroughly tired and irritable. The ship turned out to be the British India *Barpeta*, and I was to be signed on as Number 2. Once again I made the journey to the shipping office, and then down to my new ship, where I found the chief radio officer having tea in his cabin. He was a smartly dressed young man named James, who looked askance at my dishevelled appearance; but his manner changed when I poured out the story of the last few days. My cabin was large and airy, originally built for two people, and, after a bath and shave, I joined Jimmy, as he was called throughout the *Barpeta*, for a drink before supper. He explained that we were on what was known as the slow mail to the Persian Gulf. The ship stopped at all the small ports in the Gulf, finally turning round at Basra and returning to Bombay. The ports had names, but we always anchored a couple of miles out and all I ever saw of them was a few buildings shimmering in the heat haze over the desert—Dubai, Bandar Abbas, Bushire, Kuwait. The only place that I can really remember is Muscat. After the Red Sea in the *Sultania*, I thought that I knew what heat was, but Muscat had something to teach me. The harbour is surrounded by hills, and when we anchored at about 3 o'clock in the afternoon the heat was almost unbearable. One of the rocky hills was covered with the painted names of ships that had visited the port, some of them almost worn away; but, unlike those names, the two British cruisers then on station in the Persian Gulf—the *Emerald* and *Enterprise* —were in first-class condition. After a long search I found the *Barpeta's* name on a boulder close to the sea. She had been built in 1914 and had very high masts, a relic of her use as a naval radio station during World War I. She was broken up in Bombay in 1950.

Jimmy was a very decent type and we got along well. He did the day watchkeeping and I did the night. The rest of the officers were on the usual two-and-a-half year posting. Their salaries were much higher than ours and, although the atmosphere was friendly enough, one sensed that we were not working for the BI. We wore a different uniform and did not really belong. The round trip took a month, but on the day before our return to Bombay I was laid low with malaria. I hazily remember feeling most unusual, Jimmy piling me into a taxi and going to St George's hospital, but it was nearly a week before things became normal again, and I found myself in a large airy ward with a half-caste in bed on either side of me. They turned out to be railway people, and, as soon as I could start taking any interest, they both started the old cry of how white they were and what they were going to do when the got 'home'. I had grown half used to this cry from Baugh in the *Sultania*, but this time it was much more concentrated. One of them, an engine driver on the Bengal & Nagpur Railway, was almost pure Indian, but he hung on to his trace of white blood with a passionate intensity. The limit was reached when he said: 'When we were at home, before we came to this bloody country, we lived in Belfast in Northern Ireland. Do you know it?' I agreed that I knew where it was. 'Where did your father work?' I asked. 'Oh', he replied, 'my father had a very good job in Dublin.' 'Long way for him to go to work', I observed. 'Not very', he replied glibly, 'my father cycled to and fro.'

The half caste in India was indeed a tragic figure. Captain Merryleas of the *Sultania* once told me that basically the

British Army was responsible for the Chee Chee. 'What can you expect? You send out thousands of healthy young men from the British Isles, you house them and feed them like pigs and pay them minute salaries and you keep them 'out here for years.' He waved aside excuse about communications in the old days. 'They were not expected to return home; they weren't even respected by the sweeper class, which was the only class where they could find a woman they could afford. After a few years in this heat, England and home became a very hazy picture. When discharged by the Army, they stayed on; they became prison warders, firemen, and their children grew up and mostly seem to have gravitated to the railways. There are thousands of them scattered all over India, not accepted by the white class and hated by the Indian.' Years later his words were to come true, and I can only hope that during the years the white strain in their bloodstreams has become so thin that they have been accepted by the indigenous population. In the few weeks I was in the ward I learned a lot about the Chee Chees, as they were unkindly called by all the white people. They didn't seem proud of their Indian blood, only of their well adulterated white blood.

There were two night nurses on duty, one almost white named Frances Maclean and the other almost black called Tibia Murphy. These two young ladies started to make quite a fuss of me, but this caused my two neighbours to take offence to the extent of the engine driver warning me against 'those black bitches'. 'We white men must hang together against them; people like them ruin the white man in India.' But I was now eighteen, I had been at sea a long time and Frankie Maclean grew nightly more beautiful. In spite of the lack of encouragement from my neighbours, after a few nights I found Frankie was spending long hours of the night keeping me company. When our whisperings upset the engine driver, we retired to the verandah and gradually edged our way down to the dark end away from the wards. This budding romance received full co-operation from Tibia Murphy.

Within a week, the handholding passed into the passionate kissing stage, which held all sorts of promise, but any attempt to push things further was always stopped with 'Not here, wait until you are out of hospital.' Frankie wasn't ready for anything like that yet.

One night she cross-questioned me about how many rupees I earned a month and she was a bit slowed down to find that it was only about 100. For some time she was quiet and pensive and then she said: 'My father is the chief of a fire station in Byculla; he would let us have a room in the top of the fire station. If we got married and I kept on working at the hospital, we could live there when your ship was in port.' I didn't like to spoil things by telling Frankie that when my two years were up I should have to go home to the United Kingdom, and anyway my next ship might not even return to Bombay. The fun and games were held up indefinitely the next night while I was cross-questioned about how much my salary would rise in the next few years. Apparently Frankie didn't think I earned enough to contemplate marriage, and even my white blood didn't compensate for the lack of rupees. I wasn't exactly contemplating marriage, but she was an attractive girl on a dark verandah on a hot Indian night.

The next day the romance came to a full stop. The doctor said I was well enough to return to sea, so I rang the office of the radio company and told them that I was ready to go. The superintendent almost exploded with relief. 'I'm glad to hear that. The office van will be round to pick you up with your luggage in half an hour. There's a tanker out in the stream that has just anchored and sent its radio officer ashore with the pilot; the clot has broken his leg.' I said I would be ready but pointed out that I had never been at sea alone as I had not the necessary sea time to do so. 'Don't worry, I'll fix the shipping office. You just get ready.' In thirty minutes the firm's van, complete with the staff clerk, arrived, and we were rattled round to the shipping office in short order. There I signed on a tanker called the *Schwedagon*, then hustled back into the van which at once departed for the docks.

'Motorboat is waiting at steps, tanker want to go, plenty hurry', said the staff clerk. All was as he said and as the motorboat swung away from the dock wall and started approaching the line of anchored ships, the coxswain pointed out my new home to me.

The *Schwedagon*, named after the temple in Rangoon, was a small coastal tanker owned by the IndoBurma Petroleum Company and her home port was Rangoon. I found later than she had three runs—Rangoon to Budge Budge, down the Hughli from Calcutta; Rangoon to Chittagong; and Rangoon to Bombay. She was quite small as tankers go today, under 2,000 tons, but the accommodation had been built for the tropics and was light and airy. She had a black hull, white superstructure and a red funnel with a black top. I was met at the top of the gangway by the chief officer, who soon had my baggage aboard. The ship was roughly divided into two parts—the after part containing the engine room and the engineers' accommodation, and the midship house containing the deck officers' accommodation and the bridge. The two parts were connected, over the tank tops, by a long gangway, called the flying bridge, and alongside the gangway at the after end of the midship house lay the radio cabin and my own cabin side by side. By the time I had unpacked and settled into the accommodation, the *Schwedagon* was under way for Rangoon. I found her to be quite a family ship. The captain carried his wife with him all the time and the chief officer his some of the time. The rest of the officers had all been in the ship for years and, as she was a one-ship company, they just stayed until they had saved up enough money to pay their own passages home—a state they never seemed to reach.

The radio equipment was quite simple—a spark transmitter, a two-valve receiver, a 10in induction coil spark transmitter in the event of an emergency and, something new to me, an automatic alarm. This device was switched on when you were not on watch. When a ship was in distress, before sending out an SOS, the operator transmitted twelve dashes of 4 seconds duration with a 1 second space between them. If the auto-alarm received three of these dashes, it rang a bell on the ship's bridge and in the operator's sleeping cabin. At least, that is what was supposed to happen, but the alarm was very liable to be triggered off by odd bursts of atmospherics, as I found out on my first night at sea. I kept the last two-hour watch of the day, tested the automatic alarm and dived into my bunk. It had been a very busy day: a violent love affair had come to a dead stop, and I had shipped out in a tanker as the only radio operator, and all in twelve hours. I fell into a dead sleep, but, within seconds, the jangle of the alarm bell had me straight out of my bunk. I had never heard the electrifying call of an SOS at sea, and here, on my first night on my own, a ship was in distress. I dashed into the radio room, switched on the receiver and clamped the phones over my ears. There was no dramatic call for help, just the crashing of static, and after ten minutes I returned to my broken slumbers. There were no more calls from the auto-alarm that night. At breakfast the second mate said: 'Been on watch yet, young Sparks?' I replied that I was going on after breakfast. 'You'll find your auto-alarm switched off', he said. 'It rang in the night but you were fathoms deep, so I switched it off.' He knew more about auto-alarms than I did.

During the fourteen-day voyage to Rangoon I found the officers and their histories fascinating. The captain had served his time on the South African coast and was a typical deepsea captain. He never seemed to hold a conversation with anyone, not even his wife, with whom he lived in splendid isolation on the lower bridge. The chief officer had served his time in a British tramp company, and had risen in its employ to chief officer with master's papers, when, suddenly, the company had sold its three ships and he had found himself on the beach. He was to remain in the *Schwedagon* for years, replacing the South African captain when he retired, and was, in fact, the master when the *Schwedagon* came back to England to be scrapped in 1963. The chief engineer likewise spent about thirty years in the ship, and that journey home must have been tragic for both of them. The second officer had come up the hard way, via the hawsepipe, as it was called. He had spent his four years as an AB and later a bosun on a series of north-east coast tramps. He was a pleasant man but intensely ambitious, and eventually became a pilot on the Irrawaddy River. The third officer, also the holder of master's papers, had been extremely unlucky. He was a Welshman with three children who had risen to the rank of chief officer on one of the regular cargo liners operating on the Indian coast. One day his ship had anchored several miles off a coastal port to pick up cargo, where, with a falling tide, she took the bottom; she floated again with the rising tide and he and the ship's captain decided to keep quiet about it. Unfortunately, when the ship was drydocked, it was quite obvious that she had grounded because of the damage to her rudder. Both the captain and the chief officer were sacked on the spot. Jobs were scarce at home and Taffy, as we called him, decided to remain on the Indian coast. He had several jobs before joining the *Schwedagon*, the last in charge of a large dredger. He was completely bilingual and acted as interpreter between the ship's European officers and the native crew.

Both the second and third engineers had been put ashore from British tramp steamers because of sickness, and instead of returning to the United Kingdom had remained in India and had eventually found jobs in the *Schwedagon*. They, too, hoped one day to go home again.

The tiny tanker was a most pleasant ship in which to spend one's foreign service. She pottered around her three set trips at a gentle 8 knots. Even the native crew had been in her for years and regarded her as their home. The boy who cleaned my cabin and the radio room brought me back a tiny Chittagong monkey from one of his trips ashore; it was so tiny it had to be hand-fed, and all the mates and engineers took a hand in Jacko's upbringing. He grew up into a clean and healthy animal who loved white men, but hated the native crew—quite without reason, in fact, because none of them ever got near enough to touch him. His real favourite was

Taffy, our third mate, but I ran a close second. He spent most of his days round the radio room and out on the flying bridge He was loose except in port, when we put a belt round his waist with a chain on it, for we didn't want him going ashore. He slept with the third mate or with me, just where he happened to be when he felt sleepy. The wastepaper basket in the radio room was his favourite place for a siesta after his lunch. Sometimes he would tire of pottering around and race up the ratlines of the foremast, where he would stay until he decided it was time to rejoin his friends. He had two weaknesses—he was very fond of whisky and HP sauce. The saloon was quite small, with a skylight over the table and a large-bladed fan that revolved very slowly. One lunchtime Jacko was on the bridge with the second mate, and, peering down through the skylight, spied a bottle of his favourite sauce on the table. In a flash he was through the skylight, hanging on to the slowly revolving blade of the fan with one hand and grabbing the sauce bottle with the other as he was carried round. He then shot back through the skylight and presented the bottle to the second mate for him to unscrew the top. By the time I arrived on the bridge, Jacko was eating a pile of sauce that the second mate had poured out for him on the deck. The captain's wife complained bitterly, but she had disliked Jacko since he had unsuccessfully tried to make love to her kitten. Jacko picked up his liking for Scotch because he was such a gregarious soul; if one or two of us got together for a drink in one of the cabins, Jacko would always join us and have some diluted whisky in a saucer. Sometimes he would get quite tight, and chatter and tumble around until somebody carried him off to bed. The next morning he would be suffering from quite a hangover, which we used to cure by giving him strong tea laced with sauce. He was as right as rain in a couple of hours.

I spent eighteen completely uneventful months in the old tanker, the only piece of excitement coming on my last trip. We loaded, as usual, at the company's jetty at Siriam below Rangoon. When the ship was loading petrol, a tug flying a red flag patrolled the river to prevent any shipping from approaching. This trip we were to load wax into the summer tanks and this arrived alongside forward in a wooden barge, whose crew were cooking lunch over a brazier on their deck forward. The barge bumped the *Schwedagon* so hard that the brazier was knocked over on to the wax cargo, and within seconds we had a blazing barge alongside a tanker loading petrol—a most unpleasant situation. One of the sailors in the fo'c'sle rang the firebell. The oil jetty was just a trestle standing out into the river to carry the loading pipes from the shore installation, and the only way ashore was along the trestle—rather like trying to walk along a railway line by stepping on each sleeper. With the first clang of the firebell, we all jumped on the trestle and tried to run ashore. It was strictly everyone for himself, and I regret to say that the captain's wife, trying to run in high-heeled shoes, was overtaken by most of the crew. Fortunately, the barge crew threw off their lines to the ship and the strong current of the Irrawaddy swept the blazing barge astern, away from the ship. That evening at dinner the captain's wife had a lot to say about officers and gentlemen, and women and children first. I was especially singled out for attack, since she claimed that she had been overtaken by the Sparks who had that 'damn monkey riding on his back like a jockey'. Perhaps it was just as well that there was a change of ship waiting for me when we arrived in Bombay.

A runner from the radio office was waiting on the jetty as the *Schwedagon* came alongside at Elephanta Island to tell me that I was to go to the shipping office as fast as I could and sign on the *Bankura*. I left Jacko in the tanker; it would have been wanton cruelty to transfer him to a new home and I wasn't sure that I would be allowed to have a monkey loose on the British India mailboat *Bankura*. She was almost a sister ship of the *Barpeta*, I reflected on the long journey across to Ballard Pier, and then the penny really dropped. I would be a second man again, and I now remembered that the No 1 in the *Bankura* was an odd bird. I went through the usual drill, signing off the *Schwedagon* and signing on the *Bankura*, and collecting what few rupees I had to my credit from the radio company. Then I presented myself on board the RMS *Bankura*.

The senior operator and I lived in splendid isolation on the after end of the boatdeck. Isolation was an accurate way of describing our lives, because, before we sailed from Bombay, I found that my new boss was on the worst possible terms with the rest of the white officers aboard, and this included the captain. He was an enormously fat man in his early fifties and had a grudge against the world. In these days he would have made a first-class shop steward or member of parliament for one of the depressed areas. His only method of expressing himself was to lecture me on my rights. Fortunately, I claimed to have become a member of the union or I am sure that I would never have been allowed on the *Bankura*. Sailors will accept anyone for a shipmate, especially in those early 1930s when the depression had made jobs very scarce, but even the fifth engineer, on his first spell aboard, had enough of my boss after their first meeting. He refused to wear white uniform and had all his meals in his cabin, and I became a 'tool of the monied classes' when I chose to eat with the rest of the deck officers. He would slop around our deck in shorts, his stomach bulging over the top, and spout about the plight of the working classes to anyone he saw— even the Goanese stewards who spoke English got their share. He had another habit that hardly endeared him to the chief officer—he bred cats, the long lean hungry ones that had originally lived in the Bombay docks. He kept them in his room and bribed the bosun to bring him up sacks of sand. He suffered from the old trouble, which I was to meet so often—years at sea in primitive living conditions without an outlet for his energies. He was single and, as far as I could find out, had no living relatives; and so he now concentrated on putting the world to rights.

After a couple of days the *Bankura* sailed on her 'slow mail' trip to Basra, on exactly the same run as the *Barpeta*.

Again I found myself living a broken day—six hours watch at night and then two in the day. At the end of the second day-watch the curtain across the door of the radio cabin was wrenched aside and there was my bold hero 'as drunk as a lord'. 'Dun wan' you eating with those bastards in the saloon, wan' you to eat with me in my cabin for res' of trip', he mouthed. 'Cum'n 'av a drink.' For the sake of peace I followed him to his cabin. He had cats all over it, he had been sick on the deck, and the smell was indescribable. I backed out. 'Bloody place stinks of vomit, booze and tomcat', I cried. 'Why can't you live like the rest of us?' He looked at me with utter loathing. 'You little squit', he roared. 'I am the chief radio officer of this ship, and you'll treat me with the respect that's due my rank.' I cleared off. I was obviously going to have trouble but hoped that it could be avoided until we got back to Bombay—I was a great hoper in those days.

Each day some time was spent in port, loading from barges, followed by a few hours at sea. Henjam, Lingeh, Bandar Abbas, Bahrein—each one was hotter than the last. Then the boss started his games again. He came to my cabin half drunk. 'Order a bottle of Scotch for me and sign for it', he said. 'Order it your bloody self', was my ungracious reply. 'I can't, the butler has stopped my booze on the Old Man's instructions. Says my bar bill is far too high.' This really put me in a spot—upset my hero or upset the captain. I hadn't been long enough at sea to decide how to play this one. I fobbed him off and went to see the chief officer, a man I hardly knew but who at least represented authority. 'So our Honorary Parliamentary leader has gone off the rails again.' He seemed unconcerned. 'We've had this once a month for over a year now; we just stop your bar bill too.' I pointed out that it hardly seemed fair for me to go without my beer because my boss drank too much, and the chief officer roared with laughter. 'He's a member of your union. Don't you feel that you're helping all the budding radio men by preserving that mouthpiece from an alcoholic's grave?' I couldn't see this, but his only answer was to order me a beer. 'If you get really parched, young Sparks, I'll buy you one, but for your own sake we can't open the bar for you.' I went back to the radio cabin and broke the news that my bar account, too, had been closed.

With my night watches I didn't see much of my boss, who was supposed to keep a six-hour watch and then a two-hour watch in the late afternoon; but he never signed on or off in the logbook. Once or twice I poked my head round his curtain; but he was always asleep in his bunk, so I left well alone. Actually it did me a bit of good having my bar bill stopped, for the second and third officers would sometimes send a chit along asking me to join them for a drink, and for an hour or so there was someone else to talk to. I asked why the Old Man put up with the MP, as he was called, and his capers, and learned that the present captain was making his final trip before retiring and didn't want any trouble. The new captain would join us in Bombay, and he was a senior chief officer from a cargo boat and a real fire-eater to boot. Things would be different next trip, they promised me.

Bushire, Mohomerah, Abadan and then M'gil, the docks for Basra. On the third morning there the boy woke me up with the chota hazri and asked if I would 'Go and see No 1 Wireless Sahib'. I found him lying on his bunk on his back and breathing with a horrible harsh sound, his face purple and perspiration just pouring off him. The MP was a very sick man. The boy called the chief officer, who leant over him. 'What the hell has he been drinking?' he asked. 'Smells like paraffin.' There were two empty plain bottles on the settee and I smelt one. 'Is it meths, Sir?' I asked. The room boy took the bottle from me and sniffed and then burst into a flood of Hindustani directed at the chief officer. 'He says its palm toddy mixed with meths and it packs a kick like a mule. I think it's poisonous and, as we sail in three hours, I'm going to dump him ashore in hospital.' So the honorable member of parliament was carried off the *Bankura* on a stretcher, and we sailed without him. I kept one-man watches all the way back to Bombay. None of the other officers wanted to talk about my late boss, since he had never been one of them and drinking palm toddy and meths was really letting down the white man as far as they were concerned. His cats were put ashore in Basra and the cabin was repainted. The member of parliament was another tragedy of the depression—he went to sea too young and then stayed too long. I have often wondered what came out of that stomach pump they used on him in Basra hospital.

CHAPTER FOUR

Bombay, Australia and New York

I SIGNED off the *Bankura* in Bombay in September 1930, as my spell on the Indian coast was now over. The *Bankura*, built in 1912, was sunk off Tobruk in 1941. I next signed on the P&O liner *Malwa* for my voyage home to England.

My trip from Bombay to London in the *Malwa* taught me something new: The *Malwa* had European officers, an Indian crew and white passengers, and I was soon to learn that the lowest form of life on board was the junior radio operator. The radio room, a tiny hole close to the funnels, was on the spar deck. Next door was a minute box in which lived the chief radio operator, and next to that was another tiny box with two bunks, which I shared with the second radio operator. The chief was a middleaged Scotsman, desperately keen to keep his Class I ship and the salary that went with her. As we were not employed by the P&O Company, the three of us were considered by the rest of the officers to be complete outsiders. We had our meals in the saloon and we wore uniform, but in no other ways were we treated like officers. I was three weeks in that ship and the only people that spoke to me, apart from the other two radio men, were the native crew. Looking back and realising the problems of the young officers, one can sympathise with their lot. Most of them came from the training ship *Worcester* and had served their time in the P&O. Jobs were desperately scarce and their future careers depended on the reports on their behaviour that were filled in by their superiors. Their salaries were tiny, not much better than my own, but they had to supply all their own uniforms and even dress for dinner, an indignity I avoided by going to an early sitting with the other keepers of the middle watch. The chief operator pandered to all this nonsense because his continuing in the ship was dependent on the captain asking the radio company for his services again for the next trip.

The second operator was a morose character in his middle forties who had spent years as a senior on one of the Donaldson's North Atlantic liners. He had set up home in Liverpool and had two children. When the liner had been sold, he had found that all the Class I ships in Liverpool had their chief radio men, and he had been sent down to London to take a second's job. The *Malwa* was his first P&O liner. He was a typical sailor, in that his previous ship was always the best. I had become by now a reasonably competent radio man, but even this did not seem to please my seniors—perhaps because they couldn't find anything to grouse about. When we arrived at Tilbury, I handed over my baggage to Carter Paterson and left the *Malwa* without a backward glance, and with the mental reservation that the most hard-case tramp out of the north-east coast would afford a better life than any more of this P&O nonsense. The *Malwa* was a real oldtimer, built in 1908 and broken up in Japan in 1932.

My month's leave brought home the fact that I had grown away from my home and my friends: two years at sea had completely upset the standards and values I had known before. A local farmer, famous for his wit, now appeared to me as an egotistical old bore, and when I failed to laugh at his feeble jokes he claimed that I had 'grown up awkward'. I found no common ground with a school friend who had joined a bank; his idols were the senior people in the bank, and his great days in the year were the inter-bank athletic meetings where he could excel at some sport. As he explained, this brought his name and his face in front of the head men. My talk of ships, trips and places just wasn't of any interest to him. I started up a couple of long-range romances—one 20 miles away and the other 18! Riding one of those old-fashioned pushbikes 20 miles along the rough and winding country roads of Norfolk, and then all the way back again with the road illuminated by a dim oil lamp on the front forks, was the sort of treatment that one had to be deeply in love to survive for many weeks. Both romances had wilted considerably by the end of my leave, and I am sorry to say that they both went the way of my friendship with the bank clerk.

I was instructed by the London office of the radio company to report after my leave to their East London office, which was almost a replica of their office in Southampton—the windows were just as dirty and the waiting benches just as hard. Even the people were the same—a mixture of big ship men, tramp operators and juniors. The staff clerk was slightly more affable, however, and he unbent enough to say: 'You are signing on this afternoon. I'll give you your papers later.' While I was waiting, a large, well dressed man, complete with a bowler, came and sat beside me and introduced himself. 'I am No 2 of the *Viceroy of India* and, when our papers are ready, we'll hop along to the shipping office and sign on.' The 'Duke' as I christened him, then told me about the P&O cruise liner I was to join. He had been in her for two years, usually on the Bombay Mail run, but she had now been temporarily withdrawn to make three fourteen-day cruises to the Mediterranean. He went on to tell me that he usually sailed as No 1 and was in line for the next Class I ship that became vacant in the London depot. I then had to hear that he was actually senior to the No 1—Smith by name—whose low cunning had prevented him, the Duke, from becoming No 1 in the *Viceroy of India*. I heard later that because of some new equipment fitted for her first trip, the *Viceroy* had carried an engineer from the radio company as her No 1 for the first two trips, and the odious Smith had been No 2; but he had ingratiated himself with the radio engineer, who later recommended that Smith be promoted when he left. Hence the Duke had to sail as No 2 and share a cabin with the No 3.

He seemed a little appeased to find that I had a couple of years' experience, claiming that the last two juniors had been so incompetent that he had been forced to take their watches while Smith cavorted round the ship with the lady passengers. He even unbent enough to invite me to the 'Holy Place', the local pub patronised by the senior office staff and the Nos 1 and 2 men from the big ships. There I stood in the shadow of the immaculate Duke, nursing my half pint and watching the great men in action. They no doubt thought I was some country nephew that the Duke had brought to London to see the sights. I am convinced of this because a man whom I found out later to be the No 1 of an Orient liner actually bought me another half pint, something he would never have done if he had known that I was only another 'verminous junior', as he had just described his latest No 3. I found that the office staff weren't allowed to buy anything—that was the privilege of the seagoing staff. As I watched and listened, I realised that the road to No 1 on a big ship was going to be a long one, calling more for cultivation of the right people than for skill in the radio field. At last the Duke considered that he had paid the right amount of homage and bought the right number of rounds to promote his future in the radio company and we departed for the *Viceroy of India* via the shipping office.

We boarded the *Viceroy* at Tilbury. She was almost new, of 19,627 tons and with a large and well equipped radio room, but the accommodation was still poor. The Duke and I shared a tiny cabin, and the No 1 had another to himself. I found Smith to be a reasonably friendly soul, but the feeling between him and the Duke was immediately obvious. I was in the *Viceroy* for two Mediterranean cruises, the end of the outward trip being what was then known as Constantinople. I kept the middle watch, from 12 to 4am, which meant that my only unbroken sleep was from 9.0pm to midnight. The ship was crowded with passengers and, with a special cheap rate for messages to England, watches were usually very busy. The Duke and Smith were obviously proud to be on the latest P&O liner, but I was bored to death—eat, sleep and work and not a soul to talk to except two people who hated each other's guts and whose conversation was limited to explaining what a fool the other was. Smith and the Duke were tolerated by the rest of the officers, but I had no standing at all. *The Viceroy of India* was sunk by a U-boat off Oran in 1941.

After the two cruises I was signed off and again reported to the London office. My next ship was another P&O liner, one of the 'Branch' boats that had originally carried emigrant passengers to Australia but were now called 'Tourists'. The *Baradine* was much older and smaller than the *Viceroy*, grossing 13,159 tons, and was the first of the Branch Line ships to be built for the P&O after World War I by Harland & Wolff. She appears to have led an uneventful life and was broken up at Dalmuir in 1936. The accommodation was the usual shared cabin. My cabin mate was a long dour Scotsman nicknamed Angus, and the No 1 was a tiny man half his size. The ship went to Port Said, Colombo, Perth, Adelaide, Melbourne, Sydney, and Brisbane, and then retraced her route to London. The *Baradine* carried four cadets about my own age who had all made several trips to Australia, and, as they had not yet reached officer status, they were happy to accept me into their company. At each port in Australia they had friends and I was always taken along to pair off with a spare girl—there was always a surplus at their parties. The shared cabin, however, became a problem in the *Baradine*, for Angus was a light sleeper, and, however carefully I tried to undress and get into my bunk, he always woke up and grumbled. When one considers that I almost had to put my foot in his face to lever myself into the top bunk, this is hardly to be wondered at.

After a three-month voyage, we returned to London again. I still had not the necessary three years' sea time to qualify as a Grade I radio man, and my next ship was another P&O liner, the *Ranpura*. It had the usual set-up—the No 1 had been in the ship for years, and the No 2, with whom I had to share another tiny cabin, was on the brink of promotion. The ship was on the Yokohama run—London, Plymouth, Port Said, Colombo, Singapore, Hong Kong and Yokohama. In Hong Kong the radio company had a local office from which they staffed a few ships operating on the China coast, and our No 2 was replaced by 'Dusty', who had been no less than four years on the China coast, his second long spell there. He was as bald as an egg and had served in so many ships that he had forgotten their names. The local office had been given strict instructions to ship him home on the next available ship, and on the first night out of Hong Kong I found out why. The No 1 was a morose character whose only pleasure seemed to be drinking gin in his cabin alone, and I heard him and Dusty go to his cabin early in the evening. I had had dinner and turned in, and then about 10 o'clock the cabin door banged open and Dusty staggered in, blind drunk; he vomited into the washbasin and collapsed on the deck. He was a big man, so I left him and went along to the No 1's cabin, where he, too, was out cold on the floor. I washed and dressed in the bathroom and went into the radio room. By the log no one had been on watch since leaving Hong Kong, and I decided that I should have to carry on somehow. I carried on until 4am and then visited my heroes, but they were both unconscious.

At 8.0am I roused Dusty, and he eventually staggered into the radio room at about 9 o'clock. I washed and dressed and went to breakfast. I went straight back to the radio room to find Dusty gazing blearily at the bulkhead, not even knowing how to switch on the receiver. I took over again and Dusty retired. At about 11.30 the No 1 came in looking ghastly, and said he would relieve me for lunch. By the time I had finished my lunch, Dusty and the No 1 had again retired to the former's cabin for a 'livener', and, as they were still at it when 4 o'clock came round, I could only carry on. Sometime in the early evening Dusty staggered in again, so I pushed him into the radio chair, clamped the telephones on his head and retired to my bunk. The room boy had cleared up the mess, and I woke up at 2am feeling a little refreshed, but the situation had not improved. The radio room was empty, Dusty had returned to the No 1's cabin and they had obviously had a few more. Dusty was asleep in the bunk while the other one was slumped in his basket chair, dead to the world.

I had been on watch for about an hour when the phone from the bridge rang; it was the second officer, a man with whom I had hardly exchanged a word. 'Look here, young Sparks, just what the hell is going on down there? The quartermaster has been down twice in the last hour. He says the other two are as drunk as skunks and you have been on watch almost continuously since we left Hong Kong.' I tried to put him off but he wasn't having it. 'I'll come along when I come off at 4 o'clock.' He was as good as his word; he examined my two reliefs and then sat down in the radio room. 'If the Old Man finds out what's going on there'll be one hell of a row. We don't want that, it may mean the sack.' He went back to the No 1's cabin and apparently poured water over both of them, which sobered them enough to understand that if they weren't on duty by 8am he was going direct to the captain about the whole matter. Dusty relieved me at 7.55, and he was accompanied by the No 1. 'How the hell did the Second Mate get on to this?' he snarled. 'You bloody well told him, I suppose.' 'You suppose bloody wrong', I snarled back. 'I had had no sleep since you two got on this great piss-up, and he sent the quartermaster round when no one answered the phone.' Dusty came into the argument: 'It's no good blaming the No 3, it's not his fault.' The second officer pushed into the room. 'I heard that and let's clear the air. I am the only one who knows what's been going on. I'm willing to forget it this time, but another whingding like this and you go straight to the Old Man.' That ended the matter, but it left quite an atmosphere. Dusty and the No 1 carried on their drinking but in their own cabins. The little box I shared with Dusty smelt like a brewery most of the time, but you can get used to most things and at long last the dreary trip was over.

I was to meet Dusty again years later, when he was the radio man of a ratty old Greek freighter loading maize at Santa Fé in the Argentine. He was sitting at a table with a crowd of men whose skins varied from matt black to albino; he was very drunk and claimed they were his brother officers. I don't think he remembered me, although he pretended he did. He said he had left the radio company 'because his face didn't fit'. One wonders what eventually happens to the Dustys of this world; most of them probably fall into a dock in some out of the way place trying to navigate back to the ship in a drunken haze. The No 1 eventually had one party too many and was removed from the big ship class. I last heard that he had signed on a north-east tramp for a two-year voyage. The *Ranpura* was to survive World War II as HMS *Ranpura*, a heavy repair ship, and was to be retained as such until she was sold to Italian shipbreakers at Spezia in 1961, when she was thirty-six years old.

After a week at home I returned again to London to find what fate had in store for me. Another P&O liner and my heart fell. My white uniforms and my blue uniform had now had nearly three years' wear, and my salary didn't allow my replacing them at English prices. The whites especially were hardly up to saloon standard, for many trips to the ship's dhobi had given them a decidedly jaundiced look. The *Narkunda* was a three funnelled liner of 9,698 tons net on the Australian run. She had been laid down at Harland & Wolff's Belfast yard in 1914, and seems to have spent World War I, along with her sister ship *Naldera*, performing one military role after another. She was eventually completed and joined the P&O fleet in 1920, surviving until 1942, when she was bombed and sunk outside Bougie while acting as a troopship.

She was better equipped for radio than the *Ranpura*, but I still had to share a tiny cabin with the No 2. I was fortunate in the chief operator, who was exteremely helpful and friendly, as was the second operator. There was a row of single bachelor cabins on the same deck as the radio room, and strings were pulled to have me moved into a vacant one, and there I stayed for the whole of the trip. It was the usual run out to Australia and back, but I now had a decent cabin and a few friends around the Australian coast. I taught myself to type the news as the morse code came through the headphones, which obviated the necessity for writing it all down in longhand and then typing it up in a form suitable for the passenger noticeboards. The other two showed me how to use the high frequency equipment, and now I could run the whole middle watch without assistance. It was the most pleasant trip I was to make in a P&O liner; it lasted three months and terminated at what I was beginning to look on as my home port—Tilbury.

I sent off my luggage with Carter Paterson, caught the train up to Fenchurch Street, spent the night with relatives and reported to the radio company's office in the morning. For the first time my arrival was noted by the staff clerk. 'We've been waiting since 9am for you. You've to sign on at once, your new ship sails at 11.30.' I explained that my baggage was with Carter Paterson and I had nothing except what I stood up in, but he was completely unimpressed. 'She's only going to Antwerp, so you can come back and get your baggage. She always stays in Antwerp for a week.' I appealed to the union representative, who was full of excuses. 'But the office is full of bloody radio men, and I have just signed off a three months' trip. Can't one of them go to Antwerp?' I asked. He tried to smooth things down: 'You'd best go and come back tomorrow to get your gear' was his advice. I still baulked. 'Who pays my fares?' I wailed. This he promised to look into. I became aware of another man standing beside me. 'Junior, you're wasting your time; none of these dreary bastards will go to Antwerp for you and this union character won't upset the Super on your behalf. The choice is resign or come along with me. 'I'm Bob E—— of the *Westernland*. I know you've had a fast one pulled on you but there's no redress.' The union man jumped in. 'Steady Bob, I do what I can but he is a junior man and you only want a junior.'

73

Bob turned round like a flash. 'You make me bloody sick; you take the subs from these kids and the first time they really need your help, you won't help.' The union man's pride was hurt but Bob roared on. 'I'm putting him on the night boat tonight from Antwerp. I'm paying his fare and, if the company don't refund me the money, I'll personally come and punch you on the bloody nose when I'm next in London.' So I joined the Red Star liner *Westernland* and sailed to Antwerp.

The *Westernland* had an involved history. Of 16,000 tons and managed by F. W. Leylands Ltd of Liverpool, she had been laid down in Belfast in 1913 as the *Regina* for the International Marine Combine, but her building had proceeded slowly throughout World War I because of the priority given to Admiralty conversions and repair of damaged ships. By 1917 the country was desperate for anything that would float and her completion was rushed, so that by 1918 she appeared minus her liner superstructure as a transport. She was finally completed in 1922 as a Dominion liner with two funnels, and was handed to F. W. Leylands; and in 1929, still with the same owners, she was transferred to the Red Star Line operating between Antwerp and the east coast of the United States, and run in conjunction with the *Pennland*. She appears to have been the last coal-burning Atlantic liner. She was eventually handed over to Bernstein's, who added a Red Star to her white bands on the funnels, intending to use her as a cheap cruise liner—a venture which came to a premature ending when Bernstein was arrested in pre-war Germany. Her last claim to fame was as headquarters ship on General de Gaulle's ill-fated attack on Dakar during World War II. She was scrapped at Blyth in 1947.

The radio cabin was on the boatdeck, just in front of the two tall black funnels with their white bands. Alongside it was a tiny two-berth cabin shared by Bob and the second operator, Gordon, who proved to be two of the most pleasant men that it was ever my pleasure to sail with. Although both were old enough to be my father, they made me feel for the

74

first time that I had become one of a team. My own cabin was a sad surprise, just above the waterline below the crew's fo'c'sle, with a sealed porthole and so far forward in the bow that it was wedge-shaped. In bad weather, and there was a lot of that in the North Atlantic that winter, the roaring of the breaking seas was continuous, but I was young, and after a couple of days the crashing of the seas acted as a lullaby.

The biggest problem was the long walk from my cabin in the forefront to the top deck where the radio room was. We didn't arrive in Antwerp before the night boat for Harwich had left, but Bob E---- and Gordon escorted me aboard the next night. Back in London I was again noticed by the staff clerk. 'The Super wants to see you', was his greeting, and after waiting for an hour, I was conducted into the great man's presence. 'The union people have collected your baggage and sent it on to Southampton. What have you come back here for?' For a moment the injustice of the whole thing left me speechless, but worse was to come. 'You were posted to the *Westernland*, and the fact that you lost your baggage is not the company's business. You'll have to pay your own fare back to Antwerp.' He was generous enough to advance me the return fare, already paid by Bob E----, out of next month's salary. The union man was horrified when he saw me. 'But I've sent your baggage on to Southampton; what are you doing here?' I explained that the *Westernland* was spending five days in Antwerp and wasn't due in Southampton for a week; meanwhile I had what I stood up in. He wasn't interested. He had done his best to help, he was sorry that the company wouldn't pay my return fare to Antwerp, but he wasn't going to do anything about it. I went back to Antwerp with a low opinion of unions and the radio company I worked for. Gordon lent me a shirt, Bob E---- found me a razor in the purser's office and I carried on with that until my baggage arrived on board in Southampton.

The *Westernland* was on the Antwerp–Southampton run, and carried a Belgian crew and British officers. The depression in shipping was evident among the latter, for all the deck officers had master's and extra master's tickets, but had dropped several ranks just to get a job at all. The fourth mate was over fifty. I heard a rumour at this time that everyone on deck in one Port liner had an officer's licence and everyone below an engineer's licence.

Bob E---- was highly pleased to find that I could type press direct, as on this run, with American passengers, the American press was copied as well as the British. Most of it came in during the middle watch, and I had a busy time between midnight and 4am. The ship published a newspaper, and my job was to copy the press, leaving a few lines between the paragraphs for the assistant purser to type subheadings— which is where I fell from grace. In the American press there was a paragraph on a lady that had claimed a divorce because her husband had called her illegitimate. This paragraph finished a few lines from the bottom of the page, and to help the assistant purser I typed in 'This is what is commonly called a bastard'. The next paragraph was on irrigation in India. The purser decided to delete the paragraph on the divorce but forgot to delete my comment from the bottom of the page, and then handed the script to the Belgian printer, who spoke no English, so the paper appeared with an article on irrigation headed by 'This is what is commonly called a bastard' in capital letters. Then next morning the bellboy did a roaring trade until the captain bought a newspaper and found the reason for all the merriment. He was not amused and Bob E---- was told very firmly that he had to find a replacement for the humourist when they got back to Antwerp. I was too valuable a junior for that, however, and Bob conveniently forgot about the whole thing.

The three-day turn round in New York was not very exciting, for it was winter and I had little money. I amused myself by overhauling the radio sets in the lifeboats, which were driven by two-stroke Barr & Stroud engines that were devils to start. During lifeboat drill one had to rig up the aerial, start up the motor and make communication with the nearest ship. I covered the deck of the radio room with an old piece of canvas and, assisted by a sailor, lugged the whole equipment inside. Bob and Gordon, whose cabin opened directly off the radio room, said the whole place looked like a junk pile, but they left me to it. Gordon in particular was keen, because he operated one lifeboat set and I operated the other. I am proud to state that when we left the *Westernland* those two engines would start first swing in the coldest of weather.

On the second trip from Antwerp to New York the weather was particularly foul, with a screaming westerly gale that blew for six days and built up a high sea. In spite of her size the *Westernland* pitched heavily, and the noise of the crashing seas in my little cabin under the fo'c'sle was almost frightening. I finished a bout of press one morning, and turned the receiver on to monitor the international distress frequency of 600m. There was the usual background of distant signals and then loud and clear the electrifying signal that makes every radio operator jump to his equipment— 'SOS SOS SOS de SVAZ *Strathotis*. Hatches stove in. Taking Water', followed by his position. I telephoned the co-ordinates to the bridge and then acknowledged the call. I was followed by two American ships that sounded close by, but the question was who was nearest to the Greek. The signal from his spark transmitter had been strong, but ragged and broken. Perhaps the *Westernland* was the nearest? I was just deciding that we were going to effect a heroic rescue in mid-Atlantic when the bridge telephone rang. 'That Greek is about 60 miles away if these co-ordinates are anything like accurate', said the second officer. 'The Old Man wants to know what other ships are around and how close they are.' I explained that two American ships were 20 and 50 miles away respectively— 'the *Huron* says she is twenty miles south and is proceeding' The captain himself then came on the phone. 'Tell the *Huron* we'll come if she wants any help but I can't make more than 5 knots in this stuff; that's twelve hours.' I acknowledged the message and went back to the radio.

The *Huron* was busy transmitting an auto-alarm signal

on full power. When she stopped, the Greek started her SOS again. Was it my imagination or did the note seem more broken? 'Got a cargo of iron ore. Number 1's hatch covers have gone and the hold is full of water.' We heard later that the radio man was British. 'Number 2 looks shaky to me, too.' The *Huron* acknowledged and then the door to the open deck behind me opened and the captain came in. I had never spoken to this august person before. He was a short, heavily built man, appearing even bigger in his oilskin coat and sou-wester, who raised his eyebrows to see me operating the radio. 'Don't you think the Number 1 ought to handle this lot?' I admitted that perhaps he should, but events had happened too rapidly for me to go and wake him up. The Greek was transmitting again. 'The engineers say that the stokehold is filling with water; the power won't last much longer.' This time I was able to take a bearing of the stricken ship while the captain read off the gyro repeater on the bulkhead and I copied the messages. The *Huron* gave her position and the DF bearing of the Greek steamer, as did the second American ship, the *Condor*. The captain picked up the bridge tele-phone and passed all the figures to the second mate. After a few minutes he turned to me. 'Not a bad position considering he must have been without a sight for days.' The door of Bob's and Gordon's cabin opened, the captain's voice having penetrated Bob's sleepy brain. 'You take the Direction Finder, E—, the junior's doing alright with the rest of it.'

We all sat down to await events. It was a ghastly night, for, big ship that she was, the *Westernland* was pitching and roll-ing, and, in spite of our height above the sea, the radio cabin was continually being swept with flying scud. I listened to the howling of the gale and tried to visualise what it would be like on the ore ship, continually covered with swirling water. Life must be hell there. The captain echoed my thoughts. 'She's nearly fifty years old, poor old girl, with a belly full of iron ore and stove-in hatches. She won't last long in this stuff.'

The *Huron* asked: 'Have you any rockets?' After a long

wait the Greek replied: 'Yes, but they are soaked and don't ignite.' 'Too bloody old', grunted the captain. 'Probably been in the ship since she was built.' We again exchanged bearings with the *Condor* and *Huron*, and the captain phoned them through to the bridge. Then came a weak scratching signal. 'Can't last much longer, everything awash, dynamo off now, am using battery.' The listening ships all acknowledged, and then we sat down to wait. Nothing more was heard of the Greek. The captain spoke quietly. 'We have a lot of distress traffic on this run. Doesn't usually end that way, fortunately, but iron ore is a swine of a cargo in bad weather.'

When we arrived in New York, the only sign of the dusting we had taken was the salt rime round the funnels. There was no mention of the gale or of the loss of the Greek steamer. That was yesterday's news. On the trip home we had a message to say that the ship was being laid up in Antwerp at the end of the trip and the crew paid off. An atmosphere of gloom descended over the *Westernland*. Bob and Gordon were faced with a problem: they would doubtless get another ship, but would it be another Class I ship? I still had to do three months to become a Class I operator, so I was sure of another passenger ship.

I returned to London with Bob and Gordon on the night boat from Antwerp, and they were both sent home on leave, while I was posted to Liverpool. The company still refused to pay that return fare from Antwerp to collect my baggage, so I protested in a rather childish manner by resigning from the union. I found the Liverpool office a replica of Southampton and London. My arrival went almost unnoticed until I was tackled by the union representative, who had heard of my misdemeanours in London. There was a sharp difference of opinion between us, which did me no good at all, and next morning I was posted to the Indian coast for another two-year spell. The staff clerk told me bluntly that my previous two-year stint didn't alter the case at all. My goose had been well and truly cooked.

I joined the *City of Poona*, a passenger ship sailing for Calcutta within a week. She had been built by Swan Hunter of Wallsend-on-Tyne in 1912, and seems to have led an uneventful life until she was sold to Japanese shipbreakers in 1934. She carried two radio men, the senior an elderly Irishman called Leary, making his first voyage as No 1 on a Class I ship, having spent his entire seagoing career in tramp steamers. He greeted me warmly, relieved that I was not a first tripper but an operator with nearly three years' experience. He took me down to my cabin and I had a real shock—it was next door to the butcher's shop. I was expected to keep the usual six-hour night watch and sleep in the day, when the butcher's shop would be fully engaged. I discussed the problem with Leary—an appeal to the union would only be a waste of time in my case—but he was all for peace and quiet on his first big ship, so I just moved in and made the best of it.

CHAPTER FIVE

The Indian Coast

T H E *City of Poona* sailed from Birkenhead in the first week of January. The passengers, some sixty of them, were almost all women returning to their husbands and homes in India. It seemed that they had all hung on to spend Christmas at home, while hubby, whose United Kingdom leave had expired, had returned to India to prepare for the return of the memsahib. The Irish Sea greeted the *City of Poona* with a gale. The Bay of Biscay lived up to its reputation, and our passengers vanished below. The radio cabin was on the promenade deck, and, though I did see the odd hardy one struggling around, even they avoided the saloon at mealtimes, and the ship's officers had it to themselves.

The pattern I had known on the *City of Marseilles* was repeated among the deck officers of the *Poona*. They were all men who had previously held higher ranks but had been forced to accept much lower positions by the depression. The fourth mate even held a first mate's ticket. My job was now simple: Leary couldn't type and considered he was too old to learn, so I was handed all the night watches and all the press reports. The equipment was quite as old as Leary and looked after itself. Slowly we battled our way through the Bay and along the Portuguese coast; the sun seemed to have given us up as a bad job until we passed the Straits of Gibraltar, when it actually started shining, though it was accompanied by a bitter cold wind.

81

F

'This cargo of young women all screaming for a man' was the chief steward's description of his passengers, but they remained out of sight. He was sitting on the settee in the radio cabin while he expounded on passengers in general: 'Take this lot, Sparks, been home on leave for the last six months, staying with Mum, most of them; big difference from being the memsahib with a house full of servants—can't wait to get back to India'. I bowed to his superior wisdom and answered: 'That's as may be, but I don't hear any of the screaming yet.' 'It's this weather, Sparks'. The chief steward was not to be put off. 'Wait till the sun really starts shining, wait until we get through the Canal, laddie; you won't be safe up here keeping those night watches, you'll need an armed guard.'

I dismissed the chief steward's prophecy as pure malice, but the further east we sailed, the more did his words come true. I told Leary the chief steward had warned me that by the time we reached Port Said fifty hungry women would be prowling the promenade deck, and he could well lose his No 2. I suggested that the night watches were obviously a job for an older man, but Leary wouldn't have it. 'Me Bhoy, I've never been in a passenger ship in me life and I wouldn't know what to say at all. You're a likely lad and it will be all right.'

We made our passage through the Suez Canal on a warm moonlight night and, although the promenade deck was full, the night watch passed quietly. Into the Red Sea and things really started hotting up, but I still remained safe; and then, late one night, the chief steward came to see me again. 'Chiefy, when have I got to arrange for that armed guard?' He laughed. 'You're the lucky one; at the moment all the ladies are concentrating on the few men passengers, with that big German animal trainer as first choice.'

The German had been chatting with me the day before, and had told me that he collected animals for zoos and delivered them—but, as far as the *City of Poona* was concerned, he was an animal trainer. The chief steward used often to spend an hour with me at night after his work was finished, and, as we steamed down the Red Sea in steadily rising temperatures, he kept me informed about the social life of the ship. 'The passengers are sorting themselves out a bit now', he said one evening. 'The junior engineers have started coming on deck and most of the ladies have given up hope, but the animal trainer has still got a fair following.' He went on to describe the ladies, and one in particular that was really 'on the trail'. 'But Chiefy, that's a missionary going to Southern India to take over a medical mission, she was talking about it to me only this evening', I said. 'That's as may be, but she is a woman as well and is going to get that animal man before she gets to her mission', he replied. He was right.

About 1 o'clock one morning the curtain across the door of the radio cabin was flung aside and the German stumbled through, blood pouring from what looked like a wound in his neck. 'I can't stop it bleeding', he muttered. I gave him a hand towel and went to find the ship's doctor, who was awake in his cabin. 'Let's have him into the surgery', he said. 'I can't treat him in the radio cabin.' By the time I had climbed back, the German was in a fine state, with blood all over his clothes and the deck of the radio cabin; so I hustled him down to the doctor's surgery. A couple of hours later the door curtain opened again, this time to admit the doctor, a dour old Scotsman who rarely spoke to anyone. He sat down on the settee now, though with a twinkle in his eye. 'He won't die, laddie; I've patched his neck up but it will leave a tidy scar. That's love for you.'

'Love', I said, 'what the hell's love got to do with it?'

'Yon missionary body took exception to him hanging round some of the other women; she took him to task and he tried to make it up with her. While he was doing that, she took a bite clean out of his neck—fine set of teeth that woman must have.'

For the rest of the trip the German wore a high white band round his neck. I told Leary what had happened, but his only comment was that there was a moral to it somewhere, perhaps 'Do not tamper with the chosen of the Lord'.

I used to hear some odd conversations in that radio cabin. Late one night there was a whispering under one of the port-holes and I climbed on to the settee to make sure of missing nothing. Suddenly a man's voice cut across the whispering: 'So there you are, you bitch'. I heard a clatter of shoes down the ladder—the third, male, member of the party was depart-ing at high speed. Meanwhile the most interesting discussion was building up under the porthole: 'I don't care about you, you bitch, it's my daughter I worry about. How can I have her brought up by a cow like you?' the man's voice said. 'Your daughter', the woman's voice snapped back. 'You're not her father, you dim bastard. How do you think you got your last promotion, because you're a brilliant engineer?'

Two pairs of footsteps faded along the deck. I told my friend the chief steward when he next came by. 'Sparks, a terrible shortage of men and that woman has two of them.'

As we steamed up the Bay of Bengal towards Calcutta, a change came over the passengers' behaviour—they were get-ting near home where certain conventions had to be observed. The junior engineers and the animal trainer were able to get in a full night's sleep again, and the night watches became quite uneventful. On the night before we were due at Sandheads to pick up the pilot I did have a visitor; it was 'yon missionary body', as the old doctor had called her. She was a woman in her late thirties whose forthright manner and eagle eye boded ill for any malingerer in that mission in Southern India. 'I understand that my *friend*'—she stressed the word—'came to you when he injured his neck.'

I didn't like the sound of this at all. 'Well, I only fetched the doctor', I replied, but she wasn't having that. 'You know all about the whole sordid business', she snapped. 'I suppose you thought it was funny?'

'I did not know what was wrong with him.'

'You know now and so does everyone else on this blasted ship; everybody I try to talk to about it just laughs.' She settled herself firmly on the settee and fixed me with her eagle eye.

'The doctor wouldn't tell anyone. You were the only person involved and you have made me the laughing stock of the whole ship. You don't know India; this is my second five-year spell and scandal like this will go from one end of the country to the other, especially when a missionary is involved —it makes it so much funnier.'

I was becoming most embarrassed. 'It was just a shipboard romance, we have 'em on every trip. They always die a natural death as we dock at our destination.'

'It's not the romance, it's what happened during it that is going to be the funny story.'

I had to admit that it was all over the ship, but told her that the officers had little contact with the shore in Calcutta. 'There's fifty women going to scatter all over India tomorrow and this business is going to be the opening gambit at dozens of tea parties. It's not the ship's officers I worry about.' She obviously wanted someone to pour out her troubles to, and I was to be the one. She told me that she had worked her way up to hospital sister and had then done a year's training as a missionary worker. She had never had time for boy friends, the animal trainer having been the very first man in her life, and she had thought that all the usual things were going to happen, like wedding bells. She then found out that she was sharing her boy friend with at least three other women.

'I just went mad', she said, finishing her story. 'Now I have to go back to that mission and just hope that the story doesn't filter back. The religious order is a very strict one and the Reverend Singleton is intensely moral.' I could see her problem and felt sorry that I had been guilty of spreading the story of her indiscretion. The animal trainer spent most of his time in ships taking animals to and fro. Why, from the large number of women that he must have met, did he have to pick on our missionary? It taught him, anyway, that nothing can remain secret for long aboard a ship.

As the *City of Poona* warped alongside in Calcutta the chief steward was leaning over the rails beside me. He pointed to the crowd of white men standing in the shade of the sheds. 'The ones in silk suits are the burrah sahibs, the ones in Bombay bowlers, shorts and socks are the chota sahibs and they are all waiting to greet their ever-loving wives.' 'I don't see the animal man lining up with the ladies to do any waving to his girl friends' husbands', I commented. 'No, Sparks, he won't be joining any of the parties in the bar when we get alongside either. He has played his part.'

When I reported to the local office of the radio company, I was told that I was to be transferred and my place taken by a radio man who had served his two years and was due for return to the United Kingdom. My relief suggested that we adjourn to the 'Bristol' at the top of Chowringee, where he introduced me to the manager, known throughout the Indian coast as 'George'. A man in his late fifties, he knew everybody and what ships they were in and spent all his waking hours consuming incredible numbers of chota pegs, or small whiskies, which had no apparent affect on him at all. I found that my relief had spent the whole of his two years on a large tug stationed in Calcutta and called the *Pansy*. He told me that they spent most of their time tied up, with occasional excursions down the Hughli towing, or looking for dope smugglers. The life seemed deadly dull to me, but he claimed he liked it. He had a chee-chee girl friend who worked in an office and lived in the Young Women's Christian Association. 'I will fix you up with a girl friend; the place is full of girls varying from matt black to snow white, and they'll do anything for a white man if he mentions marriage.'

Back at the radio office we found that things had changed. I had to join Andrew Weir's *Luxmi* as a 'second' man again, as I still had several months to go before I could become a 'first'. I found the *Luxmi* loading at the buoys in Garden Reach. She was of 4,148 tons gross and was one of the three first motorships built for Andrew Weir's Rangoon–Calcutta–South Africa service. She was built in 1924, carried twelve passengers, and operated with two running mates, the *Kathi-*

awar and *Gujerat*. The former ran ashore in Mozambique in 1937, but the *Luxmi* and the *Gujerat* were still plugging away in 1956, which was a wonderful advertisement for the builders, Harland & Wolff of Belfast. The radio cabin was on the after end of the boatdeck behind the engine-room skylight, and had a cabin on each side of it—one for me and one for the No 1 operator, Algernon.

Algernon was another example of what happens to radio men who stay too long at sea in tramp ships. His one brief flash of glory had come in 1918, when he had been given a commission in the Navy and sent to some radio station in West Africa. The walls of his cabin were covered with fading photographs of himself in old-fashioned naval uniform—taking the salute outside his radio station, standing by the aerial masts of his radio station, standing by the generator of his radio station. From 1918 to 1932 he had lived entirely in tramp steamers, and the *Luxmi* was the first ship on which he had been given a junior. I was the lucky man!

Algernon soon made it clear that he had not forgotten he had once held a commission in the King's Navy, informing me that he was 'strictly in charge' and intended to 'run a taut ship'. When I asked him if he had picked up that expression from Nelson, he nearly exploded. We were sitting on the veranda outside the three cabins drinking his gin when this happened. On questioning he admitted that he had only joined the *Luxmi* the previous day from a Baron boat in which he had served for over a year. He was obviously raking up past glories to bolster his present position, which was why we were drinking gin, a Royal Navy favourite. I didn't like it, but was curtly informed that it would make a man of me. It certainly made a mess of me, and the next morning I swore off gin for ever. Even Algernon was very red-eyed. He asked me to take a taxi down to the Baron boat in the Kidderpore Docks and collect two small suitcases that he had left on board.

I found her a typical tramp with Scots officers and a lascar crew. The chief officer, whom I had to ask for the key of the radio room, was most intrigued when I told him about Algernon's new position. 'He's as mad as a hatter', was his comment. 'We've had him here for a hell of a long time and we just left him to himself. Sometimes he was back in the war as a communications Navy man. Then he would read some book and imagine he was the hero and regale us with the whole book as though it was his own life.' In reply to a question about Algernon's being a booze artist, he replied: 'Hard to say. The only booze on these ships is in the medical locker. He would shove some away in port, but the only effect it had was to make him weave some more incredible stories around himself. The Old Man can't stand him and was bloody glad to pay him off. His discharge book looks like a list of the hungriest ships under the Red Duster.' I returned to the *Luxmi* with some reservations about my new boss.

Soon we were loaded and on our way down the Hughli for Colombo, Beira, Lourenço Marques, Algoa Bay, Mossel Bay, East London, Durban and Capetown. There was trouble between Algernon and myself before we had dropped the pilot at Saugor. He was mentally back in the Navy, with a dozen ratings to do the work—he was the OC and I was the dozen ratings. He did not intend to do any watchkeeping but would keep his eye on what I did. I explained that I would only keep the usual junior's night watch and he could do the days. This was mutiny, nothing less, and he went to the captain. We were in the river and the captain must have blasted him off the bridge, for I carried on as usual and no watches were kept in the days. Two days out the captain called me up to his cabin. He was a large calm South African who had obviously had his fill of Algernon. 'That senior of yours is a strange character. Sounds bloody mad to me, says you have mutinied.' I told him the story and added what I had picked up from the Baron boat. 'Not having him living his bloody phantasies in my ship,' the Old Man stormed. 'Can't get him certified in South Africa, you'll have to put up with him until we get back to Calcutta.' He continued: 'Been on his own for too long; made him a bit queer. Just carry on and we'll dump him back in Calcutta.' So Algernon and I lived an odd life in our three-cabin suite: I worked at night and had my meals in the saloon with the rest of the officers; he had his meals in solitary state as befitted his position. Sometimes he would talk to me about episodes in his past which he had obviously just read up in some novel. After some days he started keeping the day watches. His logs were sometimes disjointed, but he seemed to handle the telegraphy well enough.

At Beira we remained anchored miles from shore, but at Durban we went alongside at a wharf close to the ferry across to the Bluff. Algernon vanished ashore while I proceeded to enjoy the town. I had received a letter from home enclosing the address of an aunt I had never met and informing me that she had been told of my arrival and was expecting a visit. I had made good friends with the electrician, and on the second day in port he came to me with a sad story. There was a big demand in South Africa for Burmese cheroots; most of the crew were smuggling them in, but the electrician had gone in for a killing. On the *Luxmi's* previous trip he had arranged with a Durban Customs officer to bring in a big consignment which the Customs man would take and sell at a handsome profit for both of them. In Calcutta Burmese cheroots were dirt cheap, and the electrician had filled up his stores cabin with them. All went well on the first night in Durban; the Customs officer had turned up alongside in the early hours of the morning with a light truck, and taken the cargo ashore. That ended the story as far as our electrician was concerned, but after a couple of days he had tackled the Customs man when he was on duty at the gate. A second Customs man had walked over and listened to his complaint. 'Sounds as though the Limey is accusing you of smuggling, mate. He's got no ✗ The electrician poured out his story but there was no redress, so I suggested we went ashore for a beer to cheer him up.

Sitting in the bar I decided that today would be the day to visit my Aunt, and the electrician agreed to come with me. evidence, so let's run the bastard in for causing a disturbance.'

Unfortunately the plan was delayed through our both developing a liking for the South African beer—Lion Brand, I think it was called—and it was dark before we remembered Auntie again. I showed the taxi driver the address. 'The Berea, eh? Not the area I should have thought you two would be welcome in your state this time of night', he said. I told him that it was my Aunt, while the electrician explained that although I was drunk he wasn't, and it would be all right. After quite a drive the taxi drew up in a quiet surburban street outside a bungalow approached by a curving drive. There was a light over the front door. The electrician's valour had evaporated and he thought it would be best if he waited in the taxi. The driver was for calling the whole thing off. 'I'll come down to the ship tomorrow and take you out to see Auntie', he suggested. Not for me though—I wasn't drunk and I set off for the front door using the light as a beacon. The next thing I remember was tripping over something and falling headlong into a pool of ice-cold water. It wasn't very deep and, as I scrambled to my feet, a firm hand grabbed my arm and started pulling me back to the gate. The taxi driver had had enough. 'I'm driving you two bastards back to your ship. Auntie won't want to see you tonight after swimming in her goldfish pond.'

Some days later I visited my Aunt and was made most welcome. They did tell me that some evenings before a drunken man had staggered through the gate, set off for their front door straight across the lawn and had fallen into the fountain. Before my Uncle could get out and take a hand, another man had pulled him out and they had heard a car drive away.

The day before we sailed for Cape Town, Algernon returned without a word and locked himself in his cabin. He came out after twenty-four hours and resumed his phantasies, looking ghastly but never divulging where he had been. He will always remain a mystery to me, for he didn't act like a man with a colossal hangover, and his gin drinking to my knowledge was quite reasonable. Perhaps his short naval career had been his greatest moment, and the succeeding years of hard-case tramps had been too much for him to face. He was a weird man to sail with, since truth, fiction and phantasy were all mixed up in his mind.

We arrived in Cape Town at dawn and sailed at sunset. The cloth was off Table Mountain and I thought it was the most impressive place I had ever been to. Once again the electrician and I had to get into trouble. He knew two girls who worked in town, and he and I must take them out to lunch. Not knowing the city, we left the choice of restaurant to them, and they must have picked the most expensive in town. Neither of them was remotely attractive, in spite of the electrician's claim that his was a smasher. They tucked into the food and wine like two starving seagulls, chattering together between mouthfuls. After lunch they went out to freshen up, and we had the bill. By pooling our resources we just made it, but worse was to come. They had enjoyed their lunch so much that they were going to take the rest of the day off, and we could take them home by taxi. They lived at Sea Point—a distant Cape Town suburb. The electrician's 'smasher' must have seen the look on my face, because she turned all her minute amount of charm on the electrician. 'I know you'll take us home, honey, even if your friend doesn't want to.' We took them home and then had to take the taxi back to the ship. I waited in the taxi while the electrician borrowed enough money on board to pay off the driver. I can only say they did thank us very graciously for the lunch and wished us a good trip back to Calcutta. Still, as the electrician said later, when I suggested that we had spent a lot of money for very little: 'At least they were white, Sparks.'

Back in Durban we spent several days loading our return cargo for Calcutta, and I became much more involved with my Aunt than on the outward trip. I was invited for meals and to a party at which arrangements were made for me to meet what my Aunt called 'some nice girls'. As a young man who spent most of his time at sea, I wasn't terribly interested in 'nice girls', but she was doing her duty by the family. The end came when I invited my Uncle down to the *Luxmi* for drinks on Sunday morning. He fell among thieves, including the electrician, and arrived home for his lunch in a taxi about 7.0pm. I never found out if he navigated home across the lawn via the goldfish pond, because I was not asked again to visit the bungalow on the Berea. I heard later that my Aunt wrote a stiff letter to my home, suggesting that I was heading for perdition. That wasn't true—we were heading back to Calcutta.

As she was one of Andrew Weir's early motorships, the noise in the *Luxmi's* engine room was deafening. Ten minutes down below was enough for me, but the engineers worked their four-hour watches in that hellish din month after month. They claimed that you got used to it, and they certainly carried on conversations between themselves when down below without effort; but they were all a bit deaf when away from the engine room. The second and third engineers had been in the ship about two years and had had oil sores on their legs. All in all, the engineers' life in the early motorships was no sinecure.

The *Andrew*, the Calcutta pilot brig, was waiting at Saugor, and we soon embarked the Hughli pilot for the run up the river. On the way up I made a last effort to come to terms with my boss, for we would soon both be in the radio company's office and I wanted no trouble—but he was now dreaming he was working on someone's farm and had a small ploughing problem, and wasn't interested in the radio company at all.

As the *Luxmi* was picking up her moorings in Garden Reach, she was boarded by a messenger from the office with instructions for both of us to report to the office at once. I left immediately, but Algernon ignored the instructions—he was busy shearing sheep. I arrived at the office about 5 o'clock to find that the superintendent had been asked by Andrew Weir's agents to have Algenon removed. I told my story and could only agree that he must go home. The Super had been at sea himself for years. 'I'm going to send him home as Number 2 on a City boat sailing next week, but what is the poor devil going to do then? You can't say he's mad, just odd, and if we sacked all the people in this company that were "just odd", I'd not have enough people to man all the ships on the Indian coast.' He then proceeded to give me a real picture of the life upon which I had embarked. 'The trouble is that radio men don't work for the shipowners; they usually make one trip and then we sign them on another ship, so they don't make any lasting friendships. Their work is largely a matter of listening for eight hours a day for something to happen. You can stay for years at sea without anything happening; sometimes you get a voyage where you go for days without even hearing another ship. It's a fine way of seeing the world when you are young, but don't stay too long or the monotony and isolation will get you—that's what's happened to your friend.' He explained that the real trouble usually started when radio men took themselves a wife. 'Even on a Grade I ship as head man you barely earn enough to keep yourself, never mind about a home and a couple of kids, and if you are on an ordinary cargo boat every penny you earn must go home; so you have to forgo the odd night ashore and are just stuck aboard for the length of the trip. Most ships are on two-year articles and that's a long time.' A worthwhile lecture and given in good time, but it didn't sink in, not for years.

The next morning I was posted to my next ship, which was known on the Indian coast as 'Inchcape's Yacht'—a wartime steamer with the woodbine funnel of her time. She was engaged exclusively in carrying coal from Kidderpore Docks in Calcutta to the west coast of India under the British India flag, and was called the *Homefield*. It was a dreary job. It was stinking hot in Kidderpore Docks, and the noise of loading coal and the flying dust made life difficult in port. There wasn't enough money to go ashore much; with about 150 rupees a month a few hours with George in the 'Bristol' on pay day was about my limit. The ports of delivery were usually just clumps of palm trees on the edge of a still, baking hot world, where the discharging was done by the ship's winches into a fleet of country boats that would sail out in the morning and back again with the evening breeze. Again it was noise and dirt, the only peace in the *Homefield* coming on the voyages out from and home again to Kidderpore Docks. The rest of the officers were employed by the BI and were on a two-year contract, while the crew were lascars.

For nine months I stuck this drudgery, and then I was sacked. It happened like this. Perhaps Kidderpore Docks were full on this occasion, but one Saturday evening, instead of taking our usual berth under the coal tips on our retrun to Calcutta, we were moored in Garden Reach in the river. We were clean, there was a fresh breeze down the Hughli and some of us sat out on deck on the Sunday morning and had a few drinks. It started properly, but it finished with us falling into our bunks about 3.0pm without having any lunch. The accommodation in the *Homefield* was strictly utility, and the third mate's cabin was a tiny box with one small porthole over the bunk directly in the ship's side, open to catch the breeze. Unfortunately the drink and lack of lunch created a situation which he solved by sticking his head out of the porthole and being thoroughly sick. He omitted to pull his head in again, and, when the captain arrived at the gangway with some friends he had invited for tea, he was presented with a long stream of vomit down the side of his ship, starting from the third mate's face, which was still hanging out of the porthole. The next morning there was hell to pay. The BI Marine Superintendent came aboard and posted the second and third mates, while I was told to report to the radio company. The superintendent there was less incensed than his counterpart in the British India Steam Navigation Company—'Well Chandler, you have really gained yourself a reputation. I have been informed that you will not be acceptable in any BI ship in Calcutta. I never reckoned for one of my blokes to be fired out of the BI for booze.' I told him just what had happened. 'Don't worry, son, their Old Man is a silly bastard. I've got you another ship already; go join her and forget the BI.'

I found the *Cape St Andrew* loading jute for New Orleans in Prinsep Gat, a pleasant mooring in the river. She was a tramp steamer of 3,162 tons owned by Mitchell Cotts, a South African company, and had just returned from a trip to Canton. She had British officers and a lascar crew, and had been away from England over two years; most of the officers had been with her all the time. En route to New Orleans she was going to stop at Gibraltar for bunkers and to exchange some of the officers whose articles had expired. Most of them were renewing their articles, however, for there was no sign of any improvement in the shipping depression, and the most detestable ship was better than an indefinite stretch on the beach.

I shared the lower bridge with the captain, having a pleasant cabin and small radio room on the afterside of the deckhouse. The captain was a grand old man who had been at sea for over fifty years, and had spent nine years in the *Cape St Andrew* without going home. He had been born on a farm in Suffolk that now belonged to him and was run by his wife and two daughters, and he cascaded them with letters containing farming hints collected from journals and farming weeklies. There was a sliding shutter between his stairway and the radio room at which he spent hours talking about his farm until I knew more about it than he did. I once asked him why he didn't leave the *Cape St Andrew* and retire to Suffolk. His faded blue eyes regarded me with utter amazement. 'Shan't do that, Sparks, until it's time to retire, and that won't be for many years yet.'

The trip down the Bay of Bengal, across the Indian Ocean and up the Red Sea passed without incident. After the filth and dirt of 'Inchcape's Yacht', the *Cape St Andrew* was a comfortable and peaceful ship. The monotony was broken in the Mediterranean one still sunny morning when the third mate sighted a derelict rowboat. The engines were stopped and we drifted alongside to find it empty except for what appeared to be a roll of towels in the bow. A Jacob's ladder was dropped down, a sailor hooked on the falls from the small lifeboat, and the rowboat was hoisted aboard. It turned out to be flat-bottomed with small high pitched square bow and stern. Across the stern was crudely painted *Trois Frères*. The bundle was a towel wrapped round two children's bathing suits, a bottle of milk and a sandwich tin. In the tin, which was sealed, were some ham sandwiches and four shrivelled apples. The boat had no mast or oars and was quite dry inside.

It was something fresh to talk about at supper that evening, and I put forward my theory that the boat was from a Greek caique that had sunk and had originally contained some crew and perhaps children. I based this on the distance of the boat from the African coast—some 80 miles. The rest of the officers wouldn't have it. 'Now Sparks', said the chief officer, 'you're making another bloody *Marie Celeste* out of it; that's a beach boat—it has a step for a mast which doesn't look as if it was ever used. There are no rowlocks; it had thole pins to which the oars would be secured with a loop of rope.' He dismissed my argument about the distance from the shore. 'With a flat bottom and those two high ends, she would sit on the water like a rubber ball and would move in the wind like one. I reckon some Frenchman set off to take his family out for a swim, loaded up their lunch and swimming gear, ran the boat down the beach and she just got away from him and floated off.' He went on: 'The milk is sour, the bread and ham are stale—must have been there days'. My parting shot that I hadn't met a Frenchman who drank milk made no impression. In Gibraltar the *Trois Frères* was dumped ashore into the custody of a very disinterested local policeman.

We sailed again for New Orleans within a few hours and made a fair weather passage. We were all looking forward to a stay in New Orleans: for me, and for most of the officers, it was our first visit to civilisation for a long time. Two days out of Gib I found that late at night I could just pick up the BBC, though I had to jam the headphones into my ears. It made me realise how long I had been away. At last we were berthed in a downtown wharf in New Orleans, the captain gave us $50 each and that evening the second and third mates and myself were down the gangway like rats deserting a sinking ship. We had been told that New Orleans was the wickedest city in the world, and, after a long time at sea, with the evening before us and $50 in our pockets, we were all set to find out if this was true. The Customs officer at the gate pointed out where we could catch a streetcar into the city but we decided to walk for a while. We must have made a pretty obvious mark for the 'ladies of the pavements', for within a few minutes a smart open car containing two girls drew up alongside. 'Come on Jack, let us run you into town', said the driver, a glamorous blonde. 'We know a quiet place; we can all go and have a drink.' The second mate wasn't having any of that; full of threats about what could happen to the female population of New Orleans when he was at sea, he now became quite a different man. 'Can't pick up the first women we see', he replied when the third mate and I protested about not taking advantage of the kind offer. We eventually did ride a streetcar into the city.

We found it a wonderful place, full of lights and noise and bars. In one of these the second mate, whose sophistication grew in direct proportion to his intake of alcohol, tackled a waiter about where we should find 'a good place'. We found it, too—a large taxi dancehall where they served drink and dancing at 20 cents a dance on the ground floor, and ran a brothel on the top floor. We were escorted to a table by a waiter and within minutes were surrounded by a bevy of beauties. The third mate's expression perhaps best summed up the situation: 'By Christ, Sparks, they're all white!' After a round of drinks we each bought a book of dance tickets; you gave the girl a ticket for each dance she had with you, and each girl you danced with invited you upstairs. 'Only a dollar for a short time, honey. You can give me extra afterwards if you like.'

The second and third mates soon fixed themselves up with a couple of girls and vanished upstairs, but my luck seemed to be right out. I was picked up by one old battleaxe who tackled me about the trip upstairs before we had danced six steps. Even if she was white, I wasn't that desperate. I sat

97

down and had another drink, and was immediately tackled by yet another old warhorse, who suggested a trip upstairs without even going through the formality of dancing a few steps. There were plenty of girls to choose from, some of them quite attractive, but they all seemed fully engaged; we heard later that three long-voyage tankers had just docked. After no less than two trips upstairs the second mate and his friend, Mimi, settled down at a table with me, as he put it, to do some serious drinking. His friend was quite a pleasant girl, who slipped off her shoes and turned to me. 'You wear out two things at these taxi joints, Sparks, and my feet are going first. You don't seem to be doing too well.' I agreed that my two ventures hadn't been exactly successful. 'It's these tanker boys that have cornered the market', she said. 'Tanker boys have a lot of loving and drinking to do in the twenty-four hours they are in port. I was going to bring my sister along tonight, but, when I saw that lot, I changed my mind.'

She then went on to tell us that the depression was as bad in the States as it was in the UK, and that her sister had arrived that day from Fort Worth to go into the taxi-dance business, but she, Mimi, had thought it best to start her off on a quiet night. The third mate and his girl had by now joined the party. 'Why don't you fetch her for Sparks?' the third's girl suggested. 'He looks harmless enough. Most of the tanker boys have let off steam now, and it will be quiet enough for a while.' Mimi was willing. 'I'll fetch her. She's got to start sometime; I won't be long.' The second mate turned to the third. 'I always knew he was a bastard, our Sparks, but never thought he would start an innocent girl off on the game.' The third agreed. 'The only thing is, according to the Customs' man, there just ain't no such thing as an innocent girl in the state of Louisiana. I think Sparks is scared—a great operator with those black bints in Wat Gunge Street in Kidderpore, but the white stuff gets him rattled.' 'If you want a coloured girl, I can give you an address', offered the third's girl friend; but, as unofficial leader of the party, the second thought it time to interfere. 'Mimi has gone to fetch her sister, so you can't go chasing off after dark meat now; anyway they say you can never leave it alone once you get the flavour.'

Just then Mimi returned with her sister, who was beautiful, absolutely beautiful. She was a natural blonde with a soft Southern drawl and stunning figure, and I fell for her like a ton of bricks. The two mates later said that she wasn't beautiful at all, and that the natural blonde hair was straight out of a bottle; also that she must have been Mimi's elder sister, not her younger. This meant nothing to me at the time. I bought books of dance tickets and anything she fancied to drink. After a few dances I suggested a trip upstairs. 'Well, honey', she said. 'Ah only arrived from Fort Worth this morning, and I don't think I really got the hang of this sort of place yet. Let's dance some more.' This we did and we soon found ourselves alone when the two mates vanished upstairs again. 'To stop riding up over his anchor', as the second mate explained it. Then, to the accompaniment of a number of drinks, I heard the sad story of how a girl gets on the slippery slope.

She said she had been a waitress and just hadn't made enough money to keep herself in clothes; she came from a large family and there was no help to be had at home. Both she and Mimi had been born in Fort Worth, but Mimi had later moved to New Orleans, where, according to her letters, she had a good job—so good, in fact, that she had sometimes sent money home and had at last offered to find her sister a job, even sending the train fare to the big wicked city. My blonde had only just found out what sort of a job Mimi actually had; she didn't mind the dancing but she thought the upstairs operations dreadful, and she wanted to go back to her home in Fort Worth. By now I had consumed enough drink to see myself in the role of the heroic saviour of a beautiful woman on the brink of a fate worse than death. 'How much will your fare be back to Ford Worth?' I asked. 'Thirty dollars would do fine', she replied; and I was so besotted with her beauty and her sad story that I paid out $30—nearly all I had. She told me what a grand man I was, and that she would pay me back when she had the money. I gave her my home address.

When the second mate and Mimi came back to the table, she excused herself for a minute and I never saw her again. When the third mate showed up, the party broke up, and we decided to drive back to the ship in a taxi. On the way I told them the story of my heroic and gentlemanly gesture, and they called me the biggest fool of all time. By the next morning I was flat broke and agreed with them.

It took about a week to discharge the jute and then we set off down the Mississippi for Tampico in Mexico, where we were to load asphalt for South Africa. I said goodbye to 'Nawleens' without regret, my venture in the rescue of fallen women now being a standard subject of conversation in the saloon. Tampico was just getting over the effects of an earthquake that had been accompanied by a tidal wave, and we were tied up to an oil jetty a long way down the harbour from the city. In spite of the devastation, a bar within a few minutes of the jetty had been partly rebuilt and staffed with a few waitresses-cum-barmaids and anything else the sailor might need. With my shortage of cash, I used to patronise this place in the company of the elderly chief engineer, who was a prodigious beer drinker. It was a shack without any toilet facilities, but the chief solved this problem by always sitting at the same table against the side of the shack, where one plank had a large knothole, which the chief enlarged to his requirements. 'Better than the rest of you lot, Sparks', he explained. 'You piss all over the bloody place, I only use one.' The staff didn't seem to mind, though someone did ink in some decorations round the chief's knothole. 'I wonder which dirty minded bastard did that?' he said, when I showed him the handiwork.

The locals who used the bar all rode ponies, which they hitched to a rail outside. We were always at liberty to borrow one and ride it down to the jetty, for it would trot back to the bar as soon as you slipped off its back. The captain must have been envious of the chief and I on our mustangs, for he decided to hire one for his own use from a local rancher. It turned out to be a gentle little pony with the instincts of a homing pigeon. She would carry him anywhere he wanted to go, but returned to the ranch the moment he dismounted; so I got a new job. 'Sparks, would you mind fetching my horse?'

The Old Man's farmer instinct now got the better of him, and he decided that we should have some animals on board. The ship only had an icebox. 'We'll have fresh meat all the way to South Africa', he boasted. The stock arrived alongside the day before sailing—two sheep, two small goats and two young turkeys. They were parked on the poop with a large pile of fodder. The chief mate was far from happy at having his ship turned into a farmyard and the second mate, who was in charge of the poop when mooring and unmooring, swore that he 'couldn't see the bloody winch for hay and that all the mooring ropes were covered with turkey shit'. The Old Man, however, welcomed the animals with open arms. When the last drum of asphalt had been loaded, we set off on our long trip down the Atlantic to South Africa. The weather was fine the whole time, and my job was simply listening for eight hours a day on 600m. The only break in the monotony was to exchange what was called TR—'Where to and where from' —with other ships.

The Old Man spent long hours examining his farmyard on the poop. We expected him to start pacing the deck in a smock and dew strings soon. The goats, which were quite tame, grew apace and ate anything: the mate claimed that they ate his canvas hatch covers and the native carpenter that they chewed up all the new timber he had stowed on the after deck. I actually saw them chewing coal from the galley bunker. The sheep, however, never prospered, in spite of skilled attention from the Old Man, and he gave them to the native crew cook before 'they died on him', as the chief mate said. The real interest was in the turkeys, for, as we were going to spend Christmas at sea, they were being fattened up for Christmas dinner—one for the engineers' mess and one for the saloon. They grew and grew, bigger than any turkeys

I had ever seen. I was looking at them one day when the chief mate came along. 'I don't believe they are turkeys at all, Sparks; they look more like emus to me', he said. 'Emus don't grow in Mexico', I argued. 'Maybe not. They must be buzzards then. Next time you are having one of your friendly chats with the Old Man, tell him so. Just look at those bloody great legs; ever seen a domestic turkey like that?' I did mention it to the Old Man, but he became very cross. 'Think I don't know a turkey after all my years on the farm?' he raged.

A few days later he invited me to go aft to the poop with him because one of the turkeys didn't seem too well. We found them in their run, which the carpenter had already heightened twice, and one of them was certainly unwell. It was lying down with its neck and legs outstretched, looking decidedly off colour. The Old Man regarded the sick bird for some moments. 'Looks like croup to me, I can cure that, but I'll just go in and make sure.' He opened the run door and the healthy turkey was through it in a second. It didn't fly, it just ran down the poop ladder and raced forward along the maindeck. The third mate, who was on watch, claimed later that it positively jumped from the maindeck on to the fo'c'sle head and over the side. The Old Man turned to me. 'You can go and tell the chief engineer that the engineers' turkey has just flown over the side, and also tell the cook to come aft and kill the saloon turkey before it dies on us.' The first mate always claimed that the turkey was already dead when the cook decapitated it.

I viewed the bird on Christmas morning, all trussed up for the oven. It had legs like an Olympic runner and the breastbone stuck out like the prow of a ship. I turned to the Indian cook. 'Don't ask, Sahib, he no turkey like I ever see but Capten Sahib get very angry when I tell him', he said. The Old Man was determined, though; the engineers were invited to the saloon for Christmas dinner, and the turkey was served out on our plates in black slabs. My knife just slid over the meat, and it was even difficult to anchor it with a fork. At the head of the table the Old Man was munching away, but the first mate, a rawboned Scotsman never noted for his tact who didn't believe in Christmas anyway, just held up one of the pieces of meat between his two hands and gnawed it. He then threw it down on his plate and called the steward. 'Sling this bloody muck over the side', he growled and then turned to the Old Man. 'Even that cow that Sparks tried to reform in New Orleans would make better eating than that.' That was the end of our turkey dinner. But I was a better reformer than the first mate thought. Years later, when I had given up the sea, I received a letter from a man called Ohlsen in Fort Worth who had married 'that cow that Sparks tried to reform', and it contained the $30 I had lent her.

At last Cape Town radio passed us our orders—we were to discharge the asphalt in Durban and load coal there for Karachi. The turn round was really fast; the owners, a South African company called Mitchell Cotts, must have wanted us out of Durban in short order. The asphalt was discharged in the town, the *Cape St Andrew* was moved across to the Bluff and loaded with coal, and we sailed within the week. I didn't consider it wise to renew my Aunt's acquaintance. Another long and uneventful fair weather passage was made to Karachi, where the noise and filth of discharging coal went on for about a week until the grabs had got to the bottom of the hold outside my cabin door. Then a gang of coolies, both men and women of the untouchable class, went down into the hold to sweep the coal out of the limbers.

About 11 o'clock one morning the curtain across the door of my sleeping cabin was pulled aside and two coolie women fell in, one supporting the other; the latter collapsed on the floor. There was a hell of a chattering and screeching going on outside when the first mate came in. 'What the hell's going on, Sparks! You going in for rape or something?' Suddenly he bent over the woman on the floor and pulled off her dhoti. 'Christ, man, she's having a baby. Get the third mate, he speaks a little Hindustani.' There was no need; the third mate came through the door and the three of us stood and helplessly looked as the black head slowly emerged from between the woman's legs. 'Have to help the poor little bastard', grunted the first mate, and, with his huge sailor's hands, started easing out the head and then the shoulder which followed. The third mate vanished and then reappeared clutching a bottle of whisky and a new packet of razor blades. 'A doctor's on his way, the coolies say.' The first mate glanced up. 'Give Sparks and me a shot of that Scotch, I don't know if the woman needs it but we sure as hell do. That doctor's going to be too bloody late.' He was, too, arriving just as the chief mate had severed the umbilical cord with a razor blade. The doctor was an Englishman and surveyed the mate's handiwork with amusement. 'Couldn't have done it better myself, although that's the first time I've seen an umbilical cord with a running hitch in it. Let's try some of that Scotch to wet the boy's head, then we'll get this lot cleaned up for you. You the father, Sparks?' I had been utterly messmerised and gazed at the baby with amazement; it had looked more like a coconut than a baby on its way out. 'Don't look so damned shaken, Sparks. That's the way you arrived on this earth, or did you arrive intact under a gooseberry bush? Just drink up that Scotch or I'll drink it for you', said the doctor. A few minutes later mother, baby and mother's friend departed in an ambulance.

So we had a new subject of conversation in the saloon, but it was soon pushed aside by the sailing orders that the Old Man brought back from the agents. We were to go to Calcutta to load coal for Tuticorin. The first mate was unhappy. 'I am having all the holds cleaned up, and I was hoping for another cargo for the States.' He went on: 'I was down No 3 hold this morning, and that girl friend of Sparks who had her son on his deck is back at work; three days—Christ knows how they do it'. *Andrew*, the Calcutta pilot boat, was still at her station off the Saugor; we again took on our pilot for the Hughli and were berthed in my old stamping ground, Kidderpore Docks. A trip up to the radio office to hand in the logs and extracts, and then I had the news that I was signing on the *City of York* the next day, as second operator, for return to the United Kingdom. I never saw the *Cape St Andrew* again, but during World War II I heard that she had been sunk in convoy in the North Atlantic, as was her sister ship *Cape St George*.

The *City of York* had been built in Belfast in 1903 by Workman Clarke long before radio had assumed any importance at sea, and my cabin was a tiny box just big enough for a bunk. It was located forward of the native crew quarters, and I was told that it had originally been a paint locker. In April 1937 the *City of York* was sold to Japanese breakers, the final ending of many an old steamer in the years before the last war. The senior man had been in the radio company for years. The *City of York* was a Class I ship, and based in his home port of Glasgow. He wasn't risking anything that would spoil his hopes of the captain asking for him on the next trip. The ship was signed off in Liverpool.

I went to the radio office to find that I was now to spend four months without pay, for the company's method of coping with the shortage of ships in the depression was to lay you off for two months compulsorily without pay for every year on ship's articles. For the young man who stayed aboard and saved his money, this was probably a welcome break, especially as you signed on the dole for the period; but I was always broke and it was obvious that I should have to get a job.

I knew the chief electrician to a large private house that generated its own electricity, and after I had been at home for a few days he offered me a job as his assistant. The engine house had two large Crossley paraffin engines that drove two dynamos charging up banks of huge glass lead-acid accumulators. My job was topping up the accumulators with distilled water and helping to start up the Crossley. This entailed putting the flame from a blowlamp on the combustion chamber and then pulling the engine over by hauling on the belt that ran round the engine flywheel and the shaft of the dynamo. Eventually, the engine would give a few asthmatic coughs and burst into life. My friend was ill one morning and the job of starting up the Crossley was left to me. The trouble was that I was too clever—after all, I had done a course in electricity at the radio school. If I heated up the Crossley and then turned the dynamo into a motor and drove it from the accumulators, the engine would start without the effort of hauling it over with the belt. The Crossley exhausted into a pit outside the engine house, and that pit was covered with an iron plate. The system worked like a charm, the engine turned over quite fast for about five times and then there was a mighty explosion. I saw the plate over the exhaust pit disintegrate and fly into the air followed by a sheet of flame. I stood paralysed for what seemed minutes, waiting for the pieces of the plate to return from their heavenly journey. When they did, they crashed through the corrugated iron roof of the engine house in half a dozen places. Fortunately the fragments missed both the engines and the dynamos, and when the dust had settled the engine was running perfectly. My sick friend arrived in his nightshirt—his house was close by—and I was sacked. Later he told me that I must have had about three unfired charges from the engine in the exhaust pit.

The next job that came my way was vanboy for a baker. The van was a Model T Ford and driven by an old boy with a decided weakness for beer. We had an enormous delivery round, taking bread to lonely farms and keepers' cottages, some of them miles off the road. By using my dole pay to buy the driver beer, I bribed him into teaching me to drive. The baker was quite happy with this arrangement, since he was only paying me 10s a week, and soon found that he could employ the driver as a baker's assistant while I did the deliveries. All went well for a couple of weeks, and then came disaster. One pouring wet morning I set off with a vanload of bread for the far side of the delivery area. My first call was at a farm about 2 miles off the road down a deeply rutted farm track. The wagons had made two deep ruts so I dropped the four wheels of the van into them, opened the hand throttle and sat back. The van rattled away; no hands, the job was easy! When I arrived at the farm gate, the farmer's wife was waiting; she wanted three large and three small loaves. I went round to the back of the van to find both doors swinging open and the whole load of bread scattered along the muddy lane. I backed down the lane, stopping every few yards in an attempt to retrieve the bread, but it was hopelessly spoiled; some loaves had bounced into the ditch, some was in the tracks made by the horses' feet between the ruts. I drove back to the bakery, but my excuses were not accepted. I was out of work again.

The next job that came my way was that of surveyor's labourer—pulling his chain and holding up the red and white staves. The job was surveying sites for electric pylons in the Fen country. The surveyor and I would find lodgings in a farmhouse, and then move on when we had surveyed too far away to return each evening. The pay was 11½d an hour, excluding wet time, but as it was autumn, and a wet one at that, we spent a lot of time sheltering in the nearest pub, and it cost more than I earned. The surveyor had two more labourers from the local labour exchange and within a week we became quite a team. The surveyor taught me to use the theodolite, so that I could be left to do the siting while he 'scouted ahead'. In the evening we attended dances in the local schools and village halls for miles around, and even if I had not shaped up as Nawleens' greatest lover, I did remarkably well in the Fens. The surveyor had surveyed in the area before in more senses than one and had several beds where he was welcome in the afternoons, which was his reason for teaching me to use the theodolite. He was supplied with an Austin Seven by his firm, and most afternoons, wet or not, he would vanish. He was an amazing person, chasing the girls afternoon and evening, and then dashing off to the Midlands to spend the weekend with his wife. He claimed that he was a leading tenor in the church choir, as perhaps he was; and he was certainly a leading Lothario in the Fens.

I wasn't always lucky at the local dances. One evening I asked a girl if she would like to go outside for a walk, and she burst out laughing. 'I know you have had a few drinks but that's the third time you've asked me to go outside tonight, and you've also asked my mother twice, and, on behalf of the family, the answer is no.' It was only a small place and there couldn't have been many girls.

One afternoon I was working away with the two labourers while the surveyor was about some of his afternoon business when we were accosted by a stranger. 'What the hell are you supposed to be doing?' he shouted. I explained that the surveyor was ill and we were carrying on until he came back. 'Where is the Austin?' he next asked. 'The surveyor had to take it back to our digs', I explained. He knew too much for my liking. 'Carry on, then', he instructed us, and we did. He checked my theodolite work and then drove off. When I told the surveyor that evening, he was horrified. 'That was one of our directors and a bastard to boot. I'll hear more of this.' He did. Included in our pay envelope on Friday morning was a letter from the director asking for particulars of his illness and congratulating him on his choice of labour: 'He seemed quite bright and might be worth employing on a permanent basis; see if he will accept the job for an increase of $\frac{1}{2}$d an hour'. That would have brought me up to 1s an hour, but I had to decline. The four months without pay was over and I could go back to sea. The letter from the radio company instructed me to report to their Cardiff depot.

CHAPTER SIX

Barry to the River Plate

ONCE again I joined the crowd sitting in a grubby office on hard seats awaiting the staff clerk's pleasure. At lunch three of us adjoined to the Great Western hotel for pints of beer and pork pies. 'What's the Bristol Channel like for ships?' I asked the eldest of our trio. 'Pretty bloody', he answered. 'Although the Cardiff office supplies radio men for Bristol, Avonmouth, Cardiff, Barry, Port Talbot, Penarth and Swansea, the only thing we shall get is some hard-case Welsh tramp loading coal in Cardiff or Barry for the River Plate.' After hanging around for the whole day, we were informed that there was nothing that day and told to come back in the morning.

The two who had been drinking with me suggested I came to their digs for the night. 'We're shacked up with an old bag down in Canton; she charges exactly what the company allows us—five bob for bed and breakfast. Reckon she knows as much about the radio company as we do.' I went along with them and found the digs in Canton much as they had promised. In the front bedroom two double beds were pushed together against one wall, and there was a single bed under the window. There were no sheets, just blankets. The whole place stank but 5s was all we could afford and we had to sleep somewhere. The middleaged landlady accepted me with open arms. 'Now I'm full up, dear. You can come home when you like but don't try bringing in any tarts, I keep a respectable house.' The only place we could entertain a tart was in the landlady's bed, unless one wanted to put on an exhibition for the rest of the boarders. We spent the evening in the flesh-pots of Queen's Street and left for Canton on the last tram. During the evening I learnt that the single bed by the win-dow was at present occupied by an Irish radio operator who spent his evenings partly entertaining the landlady in the pub on the corner to numberless gins and the rest of the time in her bed. Being the last man to join I was on the out-side of the second bed. The Irishman had not yet climbed into the single bed. It was a most disturbed night, for all four of us had imbibed quite a lot of beer and the only way the other three were able to get out of bed to the lavatory was to climb across me. There was one added piece of excitement when the man by the wall dropped his pipe and set the blan-kets on fire.

The next morning we set off again for the office by tram. By midday my bedmates had all been allocated ships and had cleared off to the various shipping offices to sign on, so there was only the Irish occupant of the single bed to join me in the 'Great Western' at lunchtime. 'I am to report to the office again in the morning', he told me. 'Signing on a tanker at Swansea. Will you be in the digs tonight?' I said it was unlikely that I should be given a ship during the afternoon. 'That's true, you won't. We'll get together tonight in that pub on the corner.' 'You'll be bringing the landlady, I sup-pose?' I said. 'Ach, yon's not a bad old biddy; always stay with her when I'm in Cardiff', he replied. 'She's no beauty but it's handy to have it in the digs—easier than picking up some tart and then getting shacked up in Splott. Cheaper too.' That evening we both took the landlady along to the local; she drank gin while the Irishman and I made do with pints of Guinness and bitter. 'I've put a jerry under your bed', she informed the Irishman. 'You had better use it; a body can't get a wink of sleep at night with you piss artists tramping to and fro to the lavatory all night long.'

I left them downstairs and was soon asleep. I had two

double beds to myself. During the night I was awakened by a clatter: the Irishman was standing by his bed and at his feet was the tin jerry. 'Filled the bloody thing up and was just going to empty it out of the window when it slipped out of my hand', he explained. The room was covered with lino and the contents of the jerry had formed a large pool at the foot of my bed; but, as we obviously could do little about it, we went off to sleep again. The next morning the pool had gone. Later we were sitting at the breakfast table eating meatballs, the standard breakfast in 5s a day digs, when there was a splash of liquid on the tablecloth. We both looked up and there was the Irishman's pool that had vanished overnight: it was a huge brown stain on the ceiling and just beginning to drip through. 'Go and pay her for us both down in the kitchen', I suggested. 'If she comes in here, there'll be hell to play. I'll grab our two overnight bags and get along to the tram stop.' After I had waited a few minutes the Irishman turned up. 'I settled up in the kitchen. She followed me along the hallway asking if you had enjoyed your breakfast.'

In the office the Irishman was packed off to join his tanker in Swansea. In the depression there were only two exports from Southern Ireland as far as I could see—ships' radio operators and priests. Next came my turn. I was to go to Barry to sign on a ship called the *Alban* loading coal for the River Plate. In Barry they hoisted up the complete railway wagon in a gantry and then emptied it down a shoot into the ship's hold. The *Alban* was almost down to her marks, but she was almost invisible in a dense cloud of coaldust.

She was a typical three-island tramp of the World War I era, with a black funnel and stone-coloured upperworks. I found the mate in a tiny cabin in the midship house and introduced myself as the radio operator. He took a key off a board, and with a strong Welsh accent said he would show me my accommodation. I followed him out on to the maindeck, where he climbed up a ladder on a big ventilator and stopped outside the door of a tiny wooden hut behind the engine-room skylight. He opened the door; along one bulkhead was a bunk covered with filthy bedclothes, and on the other was a bench with a quarter kw spark transmitter and a receiver. I looked on in horror. 'Where's the chair, then?' I asked. 'You sit on the bunk to work that wireless if you want to sit down', he answered. 'Where is the sleeping cabin, then?' I asked. 'There isn't one. You sleep on that bunk', he replied. I pulled aside the bedclothes, to find a dirty settee cushion underneath. I hoisted this up and lifted a board and there were the radio batteries. I could almost feel the hostility from the Welsh mate. 'What's wrong then, man?' he asked. I realised that it was no good talking to him. 'I'm off to see the shipping master', I replied, and off I went.

I had a long wait in the shipping office, but the shipping master listened patiently, and at last he said: 'Just a minute, I'll get the surveyor'. He returned a few minutes later with a tough looking character with a strong Scots accent, who also listened to my story. 'That bloody *Alban* again, nothing but trouble from that rust bucket. It's illegal for you to sleep in the same cabin as charging batteries. I'll come down to the ship with you and sort it out.' We were met at the gangway by the mate, but the surveyor brushed him aside and climbed on to the lower bridge with me in tow. He banged on a door and walked in, and then I met 'Old Dai', the captain of the *Alban*. The mate must have warned him that I was out for trouble, for he didn't even look at me. 'This man has been slipped a fast one', said the surveyor. 'Let's have the ship's plans and if there's any bloody argument you won't get your sailing papers.' The plans were produced with ill grace by Old Dai, and, after glancing at them for a few minutes, the surveyor pointed with a stubby finger at the plan. 'There's a cabin in the midship house labelled Wireless Operator. Who the hell's got that?' 'That's the fourth mate's room now', said Old Dai. 'Four mates on this bloody heap?' snarled the surveyor. 'I can't turn him out but if the radio man is to sleep in the radio room you will have to build a box outside for his batteries and then run new cables out to it. You don't get your papers until it's done and I have inspected it. It will take at least two days.' So I got my cabin on the *Alban*.

I went into the saloon for supper that night and had a fore-taste of what the trip was going to be like. The captain, Old Dai, was there, as was the first mate, always known as Yantow, the third mate, and the chief engineer. Only the last was not Welsh; he came from the north-east coast. The conversation was carried on in Welsh, but the chief engineer spoke English. 'Come up to the chain locker tonight with me, Sparks', he invited. I accepted and over a few pints the chief introduced me to my new ship. 'She was bought by the inhabitants of a small Welsh town on the share principle in the palmy days immediately after the last war when freights were booming', he said. 'The principal shareholder is a character they call "Jones the Goat". Old Dai has a lot of the shares and so does Yantow's father. They have kept her running until now by cutting all the corners and employing people from the home town at cut rates. The skipper feeds the ship, if you can call it feeding, and buys all the deck and engine stores. It's a miracle they can keep her running in these hard times. I have to calculate the coal to the last shovelful.' He explained that Yantow was related to the skipper, the third mate was the skipper's cousin and the deck crew were all from villages in the same valley as Old Dai. The second mate was a very old man who had been a captain in Chellews for years but had lost his ship, and the chief was of the opinion that desperate for a job he had signed on for 1s a month as second mate just for his food. The chief said that the *Alban* was taking a cargo of coal to Rosario and was then going to Santa Fé to load maize for Japan, round the Cape of Good Hope.

That night I had a long think, for the chief had told me that the fourth mate, who had ejected me from my cabin, was Old Dai's son, just out of his apprenticeship, and that he had failed his second mate's licence. I was going to be as popular as the proverbial pork chop in a synagogue, and it was going to be a long long time before we got back to the Bristol Channel. I weighed my chances: the union would do nothing, the radio company had not forced me to sign on, but I had

BARRY TO THE RIVER PLATE

signed the ship's articles for a two-year voyage and I was stuck with it.

The next morning before breakfast the steward knocked on the door to inform me that the captain had said I was to attend only the second serving of meals, which would solve the problem of speaking Welsh, for the second mate, with whom I should be eating, came from Bedfordshire. Later the chief engineer joined us and still later on the fourth mate, who had served his apprenticeship in a Scots cargo boat. He had become 'bloody fed up with his old man and Yantow and their bloody Welsh'—six months with them and he wouldn't remember any English. He bore no illwill over the episode of the cabin—his moving into it had been entirely Yantow's idea when he had been sent back to sea for six months and Old Dai had agreed to sign him on as unpaid fourth mate. The chief had signed on his own crew, both the donkeyman and the fireman being Arabs who had sailed with him for years. Most of them had white wives and lived in the Loudon Square area of Cardiff.

We sailed in the middle of a pouring wet night on what was to be a long and unhappy voyage. The Welsh crew members cut themselves off entirely from the chief, the second mate and myself, but we formed our own community and lived our own lives. I remember once asking the chief what the hell *Alban* stood for. 'Is it the name of some aunt of the owners?' I asked. The old second mate answered: 'Is it hell. I think she was originally called the *Albany* and had brass letters on her counter to prove it. One day the Y of Albany fell off, but they were too bloody mean to buy a new brass Y and fit it, so she became the *Alban*. True or false, I don't know, but she was the most parish-rigged ship I was ever to sail in.

Two days after passing Land's End the *Alban* ran into a heavy south-westerly gale in which she wallowed with a heavy sodden pitching motion. The decks were continually filled with water, which came over the fo'c's'le head, though the second mate and the chief did not seem much concerned at dinner. 'She's always a cow when she's deep loaded in any sort of sea, like a half tide rock.' The second mate had spent all his early years in sail. 'This isn't a ship', he claimed. 'You should have seen my old ship, the *Springburn*; she'd have been boiling along to the westward with water over the lee-rail halfway up her hatches.' The chief and I were getting used to stories of the old boy's career in sailing ships. 'Yes, all hands up to their ass in water and hanging on to their lives for a few dry biscuits', said the chief. 'At least we had fresh meat for the first week out', replied the second mate, and had no answer. The fresh meat had been cooked and hung on the foremast stays, a common practice in this class of ship. 'All the fresh meat went in my watch', continued the second. 'Shipped a green one over the fo'c's'le that put solid water up to the cross trees, and, when it had drained off, all the meat had gone.' The chief was indignant. 'Can't see why Old Dai doesn't put her head to sea and heave to until this blows itself out. Deep as she is, the props are out of the water half the time. The second and I are shutting her down each time her ass comes out of the drink to stop her shaking her guts out.' I suggested that perhaps Old Dai had a charter to catch in Santa Fé. 'We'll catch a bloody harp apiece to play on Fidlers Green if he keeps her pounding into this lot', was the chief's comment.

Back in the wildly swinging radio cabin I wedged myself on the bunk and listened to the 600m traffic. There was a voice-pipe connection to the bridge through which I passed the information that winds of gale force were being forecast by Land's End, Ushant and Vigo. The news was received without comment by the bridge; 'The Eisteddfod', as the chief had christened them, weren't impressed. Just as I was going off watch at 10.0pm the *Alban* gave a heavy lurch to port and then slowly rolled over until the list must have been 45 degrees. I climbed out into the pitch black night. The *Alban* had turned beam on and was wallowing in the trough of a high confused sea. I heard the clang of the telegraph and then the comforting thump of the old steam engine died away. I climbed down the ventilator ladder and dashed along the engine-room alleyway. The steam steering-engine was on the top engine-room platform at the after end and was surrounded by people. The chief lifted a white face, streaked with grease, and saw me. 'One of the steering chains gave, Sparkie. This may be your chance to send an SOS.' The donkeyman had rigged up a cargo light cluster and the after-deck was now illuminated—and a wild sight it was. The ship was rolling heavily and at the bottom of each roll she scooped up a huge sea, which roared across to the other side as she rolled back. The hatch was covered with a roaring cataract of water. The chief was angry. 'Don't talk rubbish, you Welsh bastard' he yelled at Yantow. 'The steering engine's all right, it's the chains on the port side running back to the quadrant that have carried away.' The *Alban* had the old type steering gear, a combination of chains on the poop and rods along the afterdeck. The poop, as well as the afterdeck, was being continually swept by heavy water and somewhere under it was a break in the steering gear.

The fourth mate now jumped into the breach. Picking his time between seas he scooted across No 4 hatch, using the stowed derrick guys for a handrail, and climbed on to the poop. A sea roared over the poop and I lost him; when it cleared he was still there hanging on to the rails. He stumbled around waist deep for a while and then dashed back across the hatch to the engine room again. He ignored us all except the chief. 'The wheel of the emergency steering is smashed and the bolt connecting the steering chain to the rod has carried away', he gasped. The chief and second engineers now went into a conference in the chief's cabin, and, when they returned, the chief gave his decision. 'The second and I can turn up a new bolt and nut, but it will take six hours, and then we have to fit it again; it's going to be a long job. I think you ought to have a tug standing by. We are taking a hell of a pounding and, if a hatch cover tears off, we're done.' Old Dai didn't like it one bit. 'You make the bolt, chief, and I'll look after the ship. If a tug gets a wire on us, it'll cost the earth.' 'The earth!' shouted the chief. 'The old cow won't be worth a plugged nickel if a hatch goes.' I climbed back into the radio room and listened out on 600m to pass the night away. I then found that there was another ship in trouble, an Italian further down the Bay; she had sent out a call for help and the French tug *Albeille III* from Brest was steaming to her position. I told Yantow over the voice-pipe that the big tug was going to pass near our position. Never mind the tug, man. You mind your own bloody business', was his only reaction.

The night wore on—the rolling seemed to get worse but it was probably only my imagination—and the dawn found us wet and tired, with the chief and second still struggling with the new bolt. It was ready by midday, and, accompanied by Yantow and the fourth mate, they made the perilous journey to the poop. With block and tackle they hauled the chain and the rod close and slipped in their new bolt. Working on that rolling deck and continually up to their waists in water, they were unable to finish the job before dark.

But the new bolt held, and the old *Alban* was slowly brought round until the sea was just off her bow, and there she remained hove-to for two days until the sea eased enough for us to proceed with the voyage. I asked the chief afterwards what Old Dai had said about that wild night and day's work. 'Nothing really. The second and I went to see him after we were hove-to and suggested a drink to thaw us out.' 'You know I don't approve of strong drink, man. I'll get the cook to make some coffee.' 'We refused', said the chief. 'Apparently, as well as being the meanest old sod I have ever sailed with, he also belongs to some Holy Joe outfit that don't drink.'

Slowly, at a sedate 8 knots, we plodded on our way to Rosario. The fourth mate had now joined the chief and me for meals, and, in spite of the wide gap in our ages, we became firm friends. The meals were meals in name only—buccalao, dried Newfoundland cod, and potatoes boiled in their jackets were the usual breakfast. It was horrible stuff and stank like pigs' dung, but the chief and second mate claimed they liked it. They must have done, for they stuffed it down every morning. Midday meals usually consisted of salt or tinned beef, potatoes, and rice in some form or another. Supper, or tea, as it was called, usually took the form of some sort of hash, whose contents no one dare enquire into. The ship was fed by Old Dai on an allowance of so much per head from the owners. The fourth mate said it was 1s 6d a day. 'If it's as much as that', said the chief, 'the old skinflint will own the whole valley you lot come from in a year or two.'

It took us forty-six days to reach Rosario. When I commented on this to the chief, he replied: 'She is supposed to do 10 knots but just can't manage it—poor coal, dirty hull. She's old, Sparks. I am happy if I can hold 8 knots without her dropping apart'. Rosario is some 200 miles up the River Plate, and once again the ship was hideous with the noise and filth of a coal cargo being discharged. From Rosario we moved another 100 miles or so up the river to Santa Fé to load the maize cargo. At both ports the chief and I managed to pry enough money out of Old Dai to get a few drinks ashore. There was little of interest there, but lying ahead of us at the grain silos in Santa Fé was a real old-time steamship. She was under the Greek flag. I mentioned her to the chief and the second mate and that her masts seemed to lean apart. 'She's hogged', grunted the second. 'Christ knows how old she is. She won't carry a penny of insurance. I expect she's been ashore a dozen times without a resurvey.' The chief carried on the story: 'That type of ship is about the end of the sailor's road; her owners are impossible to trace and her crews are people without race or nationality, literally the sweepings of the sea'.

Later I was to meet her second mate in a bar ashore, and he confirmed the chief's story. 'I am a Canadian', he said. 'I was in an auxiliary schooner that took a cargo of salt cod from St John to a small port in Brazil. I was ashore on a huge binge on cana spirit and she sailed without me. I had no proof as to who I was, so the police dumped me in gaol. I was there for three months when a tramp, short-handed and under the

Monrovian flag, unloaded a parcel of cargo out in the roads. I was dumped aboard her. I jumped ship at Callao but without papers it was hopeless; the police picked me up and put me aboard a freighter under the Peruvian flag bound for Buenos Aires. I again jumped ship, and there were dozens of us living in holes in the ground around the docks. We bummed food from ships' galleys and made a few pesos by rolling the odd sailor homeward-bound through the dock area. One day the police raided our hobo jungle and marched off a dozen of us and pushed us aboard that Greek.'

I asked him about these wanderers getting home again. 'They are all nationalities and haven't a shred of evidence as to even their name; unless the ship docks in their home country, where can they go to? They made me a second mate when they found that I knew more about navigation than the one they had on board. Their stories are all the same—they went ashore on sailing day for soap and matches and when they returned their ship had left and they were on the dock wall with just what they stood in. Anything that floats will do for a ship when you're hungry. Consuls don't want to know you. My ship sails under the Greek flag but there are only two Greeks in the whole crew.' He pointed across to a noisy table. 'There's our radio operator. He's Irish, I think.' It was Dusty, a man I had sailed with in the P&O. I tried to talk to him, but he was too far gone. 'Don't bother him', said the Canadian. 'He's been pissed for days. God knows where they picked him up.'

A couple of days later we sailed down to Buenos Aires with a part load; the Martin Gracia Bar had prevented us taking a full cargo at Santa Fé, and we completed in BA. We also took aboard a deck cargo of coal, as Old Dai wanted to sail all the way to Japan without bunkering, to keep down the costs of the trip. There was coal everywhere, even in the 'tween decks. 'How are you going to get that coal down the bunkers?' I asked the chief. 'I have three firemen and a coal trimmer on each watch, two engineers and myself', was his reply. 'It's a deck problem entirely, I can't help at all. If Old

Dai chooses to carry his bunker coal on deck, he can shovel it down the bunkers himself.'

So the old *Alban* waddled into the wide mouth of the Rio de la Plata and set off on an 11,000 mile trek to Japan. Soon I could only hear the South American radio coast stations at night, and then they faded out and utter silence descended upon the medium-wave radio frequencies. We were in one of the most deserted parts of the world's oceans, the South Atlantic. Day after day the radio logbook recorded that I kept watch two hours on, two hours off, until eight hours had been kept, but not a signal was logged. Each morning I had to fill in a book listing ships within range, and for two weeks it was blank. My idleness was too much for Old Dai and Yantow, and the latter paid me a visit in the radio cabin. The chief had used up some of the bunkers by now and all the deckhands, including the mates, were on day work wheeling the deck cargo of coal along to the bunker hatch. 'The captain and I want you to help with the bunkers', was his opening gambit. I wasn't having any. 'I'll tally cargo in port, but at sea I keep watch, and to hell with your damn coal.' 'You won't help, then?' said Yantow. 'Not on your bloody life!' I snarled. 'I'm stuck with you bastards for two years, and I've never had a civil word from any of you except for the chief engineer and the second mate since we left Barry Dock. You can wheel your sodding wheelbarrows until your bloody arseholes turn black. I won't help.' That ended it. It didn't make my position any worse, for Old Dai had never addressed a word to me except through Yantow, and the rest didn't dare to. My only comfort was that the voyage wouldn't last for ever.

One night, just as I was going off watch, I heard a weak signal—ZSC. It was Cape Town radio; the bridge of silence had been crossed, for he answered my first call. Some days later the whistle from the bridge pipe blew. It was Yantow. 'We can see a ship ahead of us. What's her name?' I explained that I hadn't heard a ship for days. At lunch the fourth mate said that the upperworks of the stranger had been noticed about an hour before. 'Which way is she going?' asked the chief. 'Her course is towards Cape Town the Old Man thinks, but it's difficult to say yet', was his reply. Early in the afternoon, the stranger was in plain sight, but she was not under way and she had a heavy list. Again the bridge whistle blew. 'Can't you find out who that ship is and what's wrong with her?' I explained the problem; I had already called 'What ship? What ship?' and followed the call with our position without any effect. Cape Town radio now butted in, asking what the trouble was. I reported that we were approaching a stationary ship with a heavy list. 'It's probably a Norwegian motorship. She radioed for a tug early this morning. She has motor trouble which cannot be fixed at sea.'

This time I climbed to the bridge with my news. Old Dai and Yantow were furious, since they thought they could have picked up the ship for salvage. 'Useless bastard you are, man, you never even heard the message', ranted Old Dai. I pointed out that the 'Norwegian' probably had contacted Cape Town with high-frequency equipment that I couldn't hear with the junk we had in the *Alban*. It was wasted effort. 'Bloody passenger, you'd do more good shovelling coal. Now you blame the equipment.' I returned to the radio room and put on the headphones, to be almost blasted out of the room by a high powered radio transmitter calling me from the motorship. She sent a long message to the captain to the effect that she was bound from Honduras to Cape Town with a cargo of timber, but the tail end of a hurricane in the Caribbean had shifted her deck cargo and given her a considerable list. She had carried on with her voyage, but now she had run her main engine bearings due to lubrication problems. A deepsea tug was on its way from Cape Town to tow her in. I passed the message to the bridge, where it was received in silence.

The Dutch tug was on the air when I put the headphones on again. 'I now have a good radio bearing of the ship and will be in his position midday tomorrow. You needn't hang around.' I asked why I hadn't heard him before and the

Dutchman told me. 'Scowegians don't carry a radio man; that work is done by one of the mates. This one only comes on the air when he feels like it. I have been trying to raise him for hours.' We passed close to the 'Norwegian'—a smart new motorship with no funnel, just two uptakes from the engine room—which had a huge cargo of logs precariously balanced on her foredeck and secured by chains. In any sort of weather she would have been in trouble, but it was flat calm.

Over the cold hash in the saloon that evening I heard that the 'Eisteddfod' on the bridge had worked up an even greater hate against me. 'Old Dai has been cursing you all day. Says you lost us the finest piece of salvage in the world, a brand new motorship. I know him, Sparks', continued the fourth mate. 'Facts don't count with him; somebody has to be blamed, and this time it's you.' The chief and the second mate were not impressed by Old Dai's ravings. 'I've seen those square-heads with their deck cargo of timber in the water, and they wouldn't have let us salvage them; they made a contract with that Dutch tug before she left Cape Town', said the second mate. 'Damn right', said the chief, supporting him. 'I saw one of their onker barques loaded down with a deck cargo in the North Atlantic, and it was an absolute derelict—water all over the deck cargo—but they were still sailing it along to Europe. Looked like a bloody raft with two masts and two windmill water pumps.' The second mate laughed. 'That's where they get their name from; they are all wooden sailing ships that leak like baskets and have to be pumped the whole trip with those windmill pumps. They're too bloody mean to oil 'em and they go "Onk, onk" the whole time.' The fourth and I received that story with some scepticism.

So the trip dragged on from the Atlantic across the Indian Ocean. We steamed into the tropics, and I exchanged signals with Mauritius and the Cocos Keeling Islands. Then we passed through the Sunda Straits into the South China Seas. At long and weary last, sixty-three days after leaving BA, we picked up our Yokohama pilot. One reads in books of sailing ships that took up to 200 days and more to reach their destinations, but their crews must have been of tougher fibre than I was, because I was sick to death of the old *Alban* and her crew. Everything readable had been read over and over again. The chief even tried Shakespeare, but remained totally unimpressed—'No story in any of it', was his comment. We, at least in the second sitting in the saloon, knew each other's business, past ships and family problems from beginning to end. There was just nothing to talk about any more and yet the first night ashore in Yokohama found the three of us together in a bar, half filled with Japanese beer, nattering away like fishwives.

Later on in the evening a trip to the red-light district was suggested. The second mate laughed and set off back to the ship. 'Better come along with me, chief, you're too old for that sort of thing.' The chief had reached an aggressive stage in his drinking. 'Too old, by Christ! I'll see these two young squirts off, and you, you old windjammer blowhard. Come on, I'll show you lads Yokohama; know it like the back of my hand,' and off we set in a taxi. It deposited us at the Honeymoon Hotel, No 4 Ishukawanakumachi, an address I shall never forget. We were entertained in a drawing room by a collection of pretty painted little dolls, presided over by an older woman called Mamasan. Two rounds of Japanese whisky and we entered into the spirit of the place. We adopted the Japanese custom of adding 'san' to our names, which became Chiefiesan, Sparkiesan and Foursan, and we were also rigged out in kimonos, Chiefiesan rather spoiling his image by refusing to remove his thick grey woollen socks and black boots. 'Always be ready to get under way', was his reason. At last he staggered off upstairs with his light of love.

The fourth and I were just in the process of setting the price and having a last drink when Mamasan came running down the stairs in a fine old state. 'Sparkiesan, you come quick. Chiefiesan no belong proper.' The fourth mate answered: 'How you mean "no belong proper".' Mamasan wrung her hands. 'I think he belong Jesus', she answered. We dashed upstairs and found the chief, still clad in his boots and kimono, stretched out on a tiny bed. Sitting beside him wiping his face was Mickiesan, his girl for the night. The chief looked ghastly, his face grey and lifeless. 'Chiefiesan very sick man', said the girl. 'He make big breath, his eyes go up and he fall on bed.' The fourth mate grabbed a mirror from the dressing table and held it over his mouth, while I tried to find his pulse. Both of us were unsuccessful. 'He's gone, Sparks, his feet have fallen down. I remember it's a sign. He's gone alright, but what the hell do we do?' Mamasan watched over the chief for a few minutes and then stood up. 'Chiefiesan belong finish. You get him out of my house. Police find him, me finish too. I get taximan; he friend, he help you back to ship with Chiefiesan.'

Assisted by the girl we dressed the chief, dressed ourselves and then, with the aid of the taxi driver, carried him down the back stairs into the taxi. We sat him on the back seat in the corner, and Mamasan set his trilby on his head. The taxi driver spoke good English. 'Prop him up, and the police will think he has passed out.' He drove back to the now deserted ship and we stopped at the foot of the gangway. The fourth slipped aboard after telling me to keep quiet. 'We've got to get the watchman out of the way', he whispered. In a few minutes he was back. 'The watchman's out of the way all right, he's blind drunk in the galley.' The three of us got the chief into his bunk, I don't know quite how. The taxi driver vanished and the fourth and I lit the chief's oil lamp—there was no dynamo in port on the *Alban*. We undressed him with great difficulty, for he was getting stiff by now, put on his nightshirt and crept away to our beds. At breakfast we heard that the messroom boy had found the chief dead in his bunk when he took him an early cup of tea. The Japanese held an autopsy and declared that the chief had died from a heart attack. There was no official enquiry, for he was an old man and there was no reason for them to suspect anything. The second and fourth mates and myself attended the funeral, but kept our story entirely to ourselves. The chief was my friend, an engineer of the old school, but, as he had no kith or kin, he was not missed except at the second sitting in the *Alban's* saloon. I always think he went the way he would have liked to go—with his boots on, and his best black ones at that.

Old Dai shifted the second engineer up to chief, promoted the third to second and the donkeyman to third. A fireman became donkeyman and his place was taken by an Arab who had jumped ship in Yokohama and been the guest of the Japanese police ever since. When the maize cargo was out, we were moved into drydock for a Lloyd's survey. We still had to live on board, although there was no light or sanitation. There was a shed alongside the drydock for the latter. All the lavatory seats were removed from the *Alban* on Old Dai's instructions so that no one would be encouraged to linger there and waste the ship's time. For some reason that was never sorted out, the Japanese ship repairers put new mahogany seats in every lavatory during the overhaul; Old Dai raged and Yantow jumped into action and removed them all, stowing them in his cabin. The fourth mate thought he was keeping them for picture frames. The *Alban* was moved under the bunkering tips and then we sailed on the next leg of that endless voyage, to Iloilo in the Philippines to load a cargo of sugar for Philadelphia.

The trip to Iloilo lasted nearly three weeks and was without interest. We missed the chief at mealtimes, for the new chief was a Welshman and lived entirely in the engineers' mess room. He was quite a decent chap, but after years at sea as second engineer wasn't going to prejudice his promotion by mixing with Old Dai's bitterest enemy. The ship was loaded down with sacks of sugar in about ten days and then again we set out on our wanderings: South China Sea, Malacca Straits, across the Indian Ocean to the Red Sea via the Suez Canal into the Mediterranean, the Straits of Gibraltar and out into the Atlantic for Philadelphia—a fifty-two day trip that was only noticeable for the speed with which the rats multiplied.

They fed on the sugar, licked the condensation from the inside of the hull for water, and were all over the decks at night. The cook would put a mug in each person's cabin last thing; it contained cocoa, condensed milk and sugar for a drink during the night. One night an odd scratching sound woke me up. I switched on the light and there was a huge rat head first in my mug, trying to vary his diet with condensed milk. The ship's cat was a powerful tom who had signed on in Yokohama, and he had the time of his life, killing rats for the joy of it all night long; his best bag was forty-two in one night. That tomcat had been at sea for years, and knew more about scrounging food than an apprentice in his last year, but he didn't approve of the *Alban*. In spite of the sport he was supplied with, he deserted us in Philadelphia. When we were discharging, a smart Swedish ship towed past us and there, outside the Swede's galley, was master Tom, easily distinguished by his two white front paws. I thought he had definitely improved his lot and wished I could have gone with him.

The ship had to be fumigated before the Americans would allow us alongside. We were put ashore in quarantine early in the morning and were returned late at night when the ship was cleared of gas. One of the quarantine officers told me that it was one of the biggest hauls of rats he had ever seen. The cargo was alive with them. From Philadelphia the *Alban* went to Charleston to load tobacco for Avonmouth. It was stowed in huge wooden drums, and the ship was down to her marks in short order; so we set sail for the Bristol Channel. I was intensely relieved, though the anti-radio atmosphere that pervaded the ship seemed to intensify as the voyage dragged on. When we had left the UK, the personal relations between the captain and myself were at rock bottom, but I had assumed that time would heal our differences. I had a lot to learn. The rest of the crew were dependent on the captain for a chance to sign on for the *Alban's* next voyage, and the Bristol Channel ports were full of sailors without ships. So they could not associate with me. As the *Alban* waddled across the Western Ocean at a sedate 8 knots, my isolation became even more complete. The poor old second mate just had to sign on again, as did the fourth mate—it was a case of survival for both of them—and to show me any friendship was almost to prejudice their next meal. Old Dai and Yantow were first-class bastards. I signed off in the shipping office in Avonmouth with relief, and set off by train to Cardiff, the nearest office of the radio company. I had been fifteen months in the *Alban*.

CHAPTER SEVEN

Greek Skipper and Spanish Civil War Trade

I HAD three weeks leave due, but there was a job to be done first. Another tramp was moving from Sharpness to Swansea and I was elected to make the coastal passage in her. I found her one pouring wet night, deserted except for a nightwatchman in the galley. He told me that she was sailing at midnight and the captain had informed him that he would sign me on the coasting articles the next morning. The ship had a crew of runners, sailors and firemen who had been paid a lump sum for the voyage to the Bristol Channel. We located the radio cabin in an alleyway by the engine room, and alongside it was a sleeping cabin whose bunk was covered with filthy bedclothes. I spent the rest of the night on a bench in the galley. We docked about 5 o'clock and by 6pm I was on a bus back to Cardiff, never having even signed the articles.

During my long absence in the *Alban* my people had moved from Norfolk to Kent, where I had been born, and I spent my three weeks' getting acquainted with the local belles. A cousin of mine who had lived in the area all his life urged me to get to know a young lady whose father ran a pub in the village. She was noted for the freedom with which she dispensed her favours. When I pointed this fact out to him, he still urged me on; 'You're only here for three weeks, lad, you haven't time to seduce anything that you've got to fall in love with. Time is the essence in your case.' Time went quickly enough, and I was making the long train journey from Kent to Cardiff and joining the motley throng in the grubby office waiting for a ship. This time I found some digs in Grangetown that were quite clean and comfortable, and there I stayed three days until my turn came round.

I was surprised to find that I was to be sent back to the radio company's East Ham office, which was not one of my favourite depots, and I felt sure that they would be cooking up something special for me. They were. I booked my bags with Carter Paterson to be held in London and set off by train to East Ham, where little had changed since my last visit there as a junior. The windows were still as dirty, the staff clerk still as unpleasant, but the union representative had on a smart new suit, and I got some slight satisfaction from the thought that I had not contributed to it in any way. He recognised me, remembering my trouble in the *Western-land*, and was quite grieved to find that I still considered I had been swindled and had no intention of joining up again. One of the listening radio men, whose manner and relation-ship with the union man told me that he was a No 1 from one of the big ships, tried to butt in and relegate me to the status of a junior; but my unending battle in the *Alban* had changed me from an obedient junior, and within seconds a first-class row was under way in the waiting room. 'You don't know a bloody thing about it', I shouted at the big-ship man. 'Just keep your bloody opinions to yourself, I've passed out of the stage when I have to go as junior with the likes of you. I gave up carrying bastards like you around a long time ago.' The union man was concerned, not wanting to be the focal point of a first-class row in the company's office. He backed away hastily, taking the radio man with him, and murmur-ing: 'Perhaps it would be best to discuss this in my office.' 'I'll discuss nothing with you until I get my fare from Antwerp to London, and I'll rejoin your bloody union when it becomes a closed shop', I shouted. The waiting room then settled into an icy silence, broken by the staff clerk calling me to his desk.

'Here's the papers for your new ship and a letter explaining what you are to do. Now for Christ's sake get on your way before they start breaking up the waiting room furniture.' I took the papers and stamped out of the depot, feeling that the foot of my ladder to fame in the radio company was not set in the London depot.

I read my instructions on the pavement outside and found that I had to report to an office in St Mary Axe to meet the captain of the *Katerina*, my next ship. My new captain was a harassed little man who seemed pleased at the chance to unload some of his troubles, and we adjourned to the nearest Lyons to talk about them. Captain Poulous was a Greek, and worked for a small shipping company in Rhodes that had recently bought an old ship laid up in the Blackwater River, where she had been for four years. He explained that she had previously belonged to a hard-case north-east-coast tramp company, which had laid her up when the depression really started, that she was now the *Katerina* and that he had to get her round to Port Talbot with a crew of runners. He said he had never seen the *Katerina*, but he had seen her specifications: she was a World War I standard ship, and she had been called the 'War Something' when she was launched. The chief engineer, the first mate and the owner were due the next day. Poulous had a heap of woe—the *Katerina* had just swung on her hook for four years, and it would cost the earth to get her ready for sea and then round to Port Talbot in time to load a cargo of coal for Rio. I was inclined to agree with him. Once again the London depot of the radio company had done me proud, for the *Katerina* must have been at least twenty-five years old.

The next morning we all met in St Mary Axe, and a motley crew we were. The chief officer was a Belgian, the chief engineer was from Mauritius and the rest of the crew were all Greeks whom we were to pick up in Port Talbot. Little Poulous explained that he had hired a tug in Ipswich that would take us out to the *Katerina* and stand by until we got the old lady under way.

The Blackwater was full of laid-up tramps swinging drearily at their moorings. Some appeared to have shipkeepers on board, but the rest looked completely neglected, and the most neglected of all was my new ship. The only clean thing about her was her name, crudely painted on her bows and across her old-fashioned stern—Captain Poulous had had that done by shore labour, but he hadn't told them how to spell her new port of registry, and they had spelt Rhodes as Roads. It was late afternoon when the tug edged in to the pilot ladder that dangled down the *Katerina's* rusty side and I could look at her closely. She was empty and high in the water and her sides were coated with rust, as was her propeller, and the funnel was just a rusty pipe streaked with bird manure. The old *Alban* had looked like a liner in comparison. When we climbed on deck we found that it was covered with grass.

The four of us set to, hauling up the stores from the tug and stowing them in the galley, which showed signs of recent occupation. I guessed the painters had used it for brewing tea. The chief vanished down the engine room ladder, while I searched around for the radio cabin. It was a little box clamped behind the engine-room skylight, divided into two rooms. The radio-room door was warped shut, and this had kept out the worst of the weather, but the door of the sleeping cabin had been left swinging in the wind, and the bunk was full of mouldy bedclothes that had been rotting away for four years. The small settee cushion had just crumbled away. Eventually I cleaned it out with a shovel from the stokehold. Poor old Poulous was running round his new command like a man demented. The chief engineer reported that it would take a week to get the engine running, and the chief officer that the ship had been robbed completely bare, not even an empty paint tin remaining. And the owner wanted the ship to sail for Port Talbot in the morning.

Fortunately the galley bunker was full of coal, and we all spent the evening and night on the galley benches. Captain Poulous fried up eggs and bacon for supper, and we took turns using a broken fork and the chief officer's pocket knife. It was a good job it was summertime.

The next morning the owner arrived. Bedding, food, water, ropes and a crew of runners—his face got longer and longer as the day went on and more and more stores had to be brought from ashore. 'I buy ship ready to sail, her previous owners tell me, but I find ship with noddings on board.' 'Her previous owners were the hungriest gutted collection of dog robbers that ever had a ship', I said, but he didn't take much comfort from that remark. A new set of accumulators arrived from the radio company, and I was amazed to find that the receiver was still working in spite of its open air treatment. I could not check the transmitter until the chief had his dynamo running again.

It was useless to stand on my dignity as an officer in a ship in such desperate need of manual labour, and I turned to with the chief officer to help where I could. My first job was to unblock the whistle-pipe from the bridge to the engine room, which entailed climbing into the 'tween decks and dismantling lots of rusty iron pipe. My next was to help the chief engineer with his dynamo. When at last we had some steam on the engine that turned the dynamo, the chief and I stood ready for our testing session. The dynamo started with a hideous squealing and was immediately stopped; we found a rat's nest complete with baby rats between the pole pieces. Meanwhile we still lived in the galley and Captain Poulous was still the cook. After my dynamo job, the chief and I joined the mate in struggling with the windlass. The ship had two anchors down and the chain cables were literally knotted together; it took the mate three days to raise one anchor up to the hawsepipe and to have the other in the water ready to be picked up when we were set to sail. Meanwhile I became a skilled windlass operator.

As the days went by the owner and Poulous aged before our eyes, since there is nothing like money dribbling away to age a Greek. After ten days the chief had his ancient coffee-grinder of an engine turning over, and, with the mate on the fo'c'sle, Poulous at the wheel, and me at the windlass, we edged up to our anchor from the water. Slowly the big muddy links of chain dropped into the locker below and then the mate called: 'She's up and down'. Very slowly the *Katerina* moved down the Blackwater to the sea. The radio transmitter worked after a few false starts, and I solved our lack of a call sign by using the one she had had when under the British flag. Halfway down the channel we ran into fog and our troubles started. The chief complained that the engine nearly stopped every time the whistle was blown. The mate, who was navigating, knew that the compasses were widely out. In an hour we drifted to a halt when the mate rang down to stop the engines. We were completely lost.

I had been acting as bridge lookout, and I suggested to Poulous and the mate that I got them some radio bearings. In those days a radio bearing from a British Coast station cost 5s and Poulous' face fell. 'The only call sign I have is the British one, so that the original owners will get the bill. Let them put it against what they robbed you of.' Poulous thought this good business and, after getting the chief engineer to stand by the dynamo, I cranked up the old spark transmitter. Niton, Land's End and Ushant all gave me bearings, which the mate and I plotted in the chartroom on the lower bridge; but the fix he had plotted on the chart gave us the horrors, for it placed us less than a mile from the Isle of Wight. 'All that's done is to frighten us, Sparks. Could we possibly be set in there?' asked the mate. We returned to the upper bridge, where Poulous met us with his usual harried frown. 'Where did it put us?' he asked. 'Ashore', said the mate. 'Right amongst the bathers on the Isle of Wight.'

The three of us stood in the middle of the old-fashioned open bridge and suddenly became aware of the silence. Half an hour earlier we had been surrounded by the hooting and roaring of the usual Channel traffic fog signals, but now all was still. Suddenly a loud voice seemed to roar from under our feet: 'You're bloody close in, Skipper. Ought to get further out or you'll be on the beach.' We all rushed to the wing of the bridge, to see an open pleasure craft below. 'How far are we out?' I asked the man in the stern. 'About half a mile', he replied. I yelled our thanks while the mate was ringing the telegraph for full ahead and Poulous was spinning the old-fashioned wheel over. As the *Katerina* edged away on a southerly heading the fog lightened, and twenty minutes later we burst into brilliant sunshine. A strong breeze was rolling the fog up channel. 'Have to do the rest of the navigation by eye', said the mate. 'The compasses must be, as Sparks says, right up the bloody crick.' The rest of the trip was coast-crawling until we were in the Bristol Channel and could see the Welsh coast. Twice during the night I produced radio bearings to confirm our position, and late the next afternoon we picked up the Port Talbot pilot. The ship was drydocked and the hull scraped, while the Greek crew and the rest of the officers arrived.

I asked Poulous if I was supposed to sign on for the next trip, as we had only coasting articles for the trip round from the Blackwater, and the owner heard me. 'Oh yes, Mr Sparks, captain want you to sign on my sheep; your wages too high but I can't get Greek radio man.' He always referred to the 'War Whatnot', as I called her, as 'my sheep'. The second mate turned out to be the owner's teenage nephew. 'I don't want you leading him to the girls, Mr Sparks.' I denied that anything of the sort would happen. 'Yes, but look how you take my sheep in to see the girls in the Hinglish Channel.' Soon we were under the coal tips and the owner departed for Rhodes. He wasn't a bad little chap, for, after he left, three Lloyd Loom chairs were delivered on board for the chief, the mate and myself, mine labelled 'Mr Sparks'.

Soon the *Katerina* was down to her marks with best Welsh steam coal and waddling out into the Bristol Channel to set course for Rio de Janeiro. Perhaps because of my help in the early days of the trip, I found that I was welcomed on board as a real crew member—an unusual experience. As there were only two mates, they were always keen to let me take a watch on the bridge and release them for other jobs around the ship, of which there were many. I became particularly friendly with the Belgian mate, who bit by bit told me about his seagoing career. Albert Smit had been a chief officer in a Belgian company that traded between Antwerp and what was originally the Belgian Congo, and well up the promotion ladder when he ran right out of luck. He was on the bridge in the English Channel, howeward-bound from the Congo, when they ran into a fogbank. It was just dawn and the fog seemed to be moving rapidly, with visibility varying between a mile and zero. The hooters and whistles of other ships were muffled or amplified in the most disconcerting manner, and Smit admitted that the whole situation was confusing in the extreme. He had stopped engines and was steadily blowing his whistle when a French tanker plunged out of the fogbank into the fore part of his ship. Both ships were so badly damaged that tugs had to be summoned to tow them into Brest.

Smit said the enquiry was a shambles. The Frenchman denied he was at half speed, claiming that Smit was stopped in the water but not blowing his whistle, and the blame was apportioned fifty-fifty. It was the end of Smit's career in the Belgium Mail company, and he joined the thousands of unemployed sailors in the Antwerp Docks, amongst whom his Belgian master's papers only made him suspect. His stories of the ships in which he had sailed since then would make a book in their own right. The story that sticks in my mind was about an ancient steamer owned by an Arab Company in Algiers. She was loaded with a cargo of cement for Perim, at the southern end of the Red Sea, and he joined her as master in Bougie, North Africa. He found the rest of the officers and crew were typical Mediterranean flotsam, but what really surprised him was that the second mate claimed to be the owner. After passing through the Suez Canal, the second mate took over, with the full co-operation of the rest of the crew, and Smit found that he was master in less than name only. They passed Perim and sailed south into the Indian Ocean, well clear of the Straits, and then back for the coast of Saudi Arabia. There they were met by a dhow, which piloted them behind a reef where the ship could anchor and discharge the 'cement'. Smit said it was packed in long flat boxes, which he considered an expensive way to transport cement. Soon the ship was surrounded by a fleet of dhows into which the rifles and ammunition in the 'cement' boxes were discharged. Smit went to the second mate. 'Okay, so you used my papers to get your ship through the Canal. Now what happens to me?' The second-mate-cum-owner was a French Syrian, Smit thought, and he had a simple answer to that problem: 'We dump you aboard the last dhow, and then we are going back to the Dutch East Indies. That's where I joined her originally, but we don't want another captain.'

Smit's gear was slung on to the last dhow and he became a dhow deckhand. The guns were put ashore somewhere on the Trucial Oman Coast, and the dhow was loaded with hides for East Africa. Smit said the Arab skipper of the dhow had a compass, a few old blueback charts and an incredible knowledge of the sea and his position. In the three months it took to reach Kilindini, Smit taught the skipper English and gradually found out that the old man had some knowledge of fixing his position from the stars. He said his father had taught him, and also showed Smit some books in Arabic that he said were on astro-navigation. The old skipper was worried about British reaction to a European among his crew, and he put Smit ashore in a dugout about 20 miles north of Kilindini. Smit's was a long story of prisons, hard-case tramps and ships under odd flags of convenience from that coral strand to the old *Katerina*.

In spite of the Greek flag, the polygot crew of the old steamer made English their common language, and Poulous and Smit decided that regardless of the fact that I was signed on as a radio operator I became unofficial third mate, while the second mate worked around the decks with the crew. He didn't mind; his English was fragmentary, so, while I taught him English, Poulous and Smit taught me navigation. Wireless was not used very much in the *Katerina*. The ship was old and slow and the food awful, but I was very happy in that old war boat, perhaps, I have often thought, because I was the only one drawing a salary; the rest, including Smit, were signed on for their food and accommodation.

One morning after breakfast I adjourned to the top bridge and leaned on the rail beside Smit. It was a beautiful tropical morning with a sea like glass, and ahead of us was a ship. Smit was watching her carefully. 'Sparks, I thought we were the slowest ship at sea but, by God, we're overhauling her!' Poulous came and leaned over the rail beside me, and he had heard Smit's remark. 'She must be stopped if we are overhauling her.' He was right. As we drew closer, we could see that she was apparently in perfect trim; there was a slight haze of smoke from her funnel but not a ripple under her stern. Poulous vanished down the ladder and returned with a long brass telescope, which he handed to Smit. 'You see him best, Mister.' Smit put the brass tube to his eye, and after some fiddling said: 'It's old, but it's a bloody good telescope, Skipper. Just can't read her name, though, even at this distance'. He fiddled some more, watched impatiently by the skipper and myself. 'Yeah, she's the *Baron Elcho* of Glasgow and she's stopped.' I dashed off the bridge to the radio cabin and looked up the call sign of the *Baron Elcho*; then I slowly started up the old rotary gap discharge transmitter and keyed it out. I did this three times without reply, and then dashed back to the bridge to tell the mate and Poulous of my failure.

'It's one of the Hungry Hughies all right', said Smit. 'I've heard of Hungry Hogarth's ships', said Poulous. 'Perhaps they all die of starvation.' I laughed. 'Hogarth's have Scotch crews and they are only used to porridge. Take a long time to starve them out.' Meanwhile the mate was busy making a speaking trumpet out of a cardboard box that the steward had produced. Soon we were close enough to see that there was apparently nothing wrong with the Baron boat, and that there were several officers on the bridge. 'Don't look too excited, Sparks', Smit said, 'I feel that she has stopped for repairs in the engine room, and this isn't the wonderful salvage case where we all make a fortune. Give them a hail and see what's wrong.' I leant out of the wing of the bridge. 'Want any help?' I shouted through the home-made megaphone. A gentleman in a Bombay bowler came to the cab of the *Baron Elcho's* bridge complete with a megaphone. 'Nay, just wee bittee trouble down below. Be on our way in an oor.' 'Sure you don't want a pull', I yelled back. 'Yee couldna pull a black man off his sister in that old rust bucket. On your way, laddie.' Poulous pulled the telegraph to 'full ahead' and the *Katerina* surged away for Rio. 'If ever we stop long enough, I'll buy some paint out of my own pocket and paint that bloody funnel myself,' said the mate. Poulous laughed. 'What pocket, Mister Mate? I like it best how Sparks described it. Clever word, that.' 'Scabrous' was the word I had used.

The *Katerina* arrived in Rio harbour early one morning. From my position at the windlass I could see the harbour at its best, and I thought it the most beautiful place I had ever visited. I said so to Smit, who was in charge of the fo'c'sle. 'Not a bad place, Rio', he replied. 'People speak Portuguese and are as mixed up in colour as you can imagine—matt black to white—and they have an incredibly cheap booze called cana.' Today, I suppose, Smit would have said they were completely integrated. The pilot anchored us at Niteroi, and Poulous went ashore to receive his orders. Several days earlier I had called the radio station at Rio using the ship's full name as a call sign, and asked if they had orders, but, if they had, they wouldn't pass them on. At lunchtime Poulous returned in a shore boat, climbed up to the bridge and then broke the news. 'We gotta take this coal cargo on, it was sold when we were at sea. We gotta take it to Punta Arenas.' Smit roared with laughter. 'Of all the bloody awful places to go; only thing any good in that bloody hole is the fresh mutton.' He then explained that it was in the Magellan Straits behind Cape Horn, and that he had been there years before with a cargo of coal. 'Most sailors call it Sandy Point', he said.

The next day we went alongside and took on bunkers for the run south, while Poulous went ashore for some fresh charts. The ship spent three hours coaling, and then returned to her anchorage. It was years before I was to revisit Rio and find out if it lived up to my first expectations. Late that evening we sailed off through that wonderful harbour bound for Punta Arenas. The weather steadily grew colder as we went south and soon my bridge coat, which had seen no active service for years, was being used on the night watches.

After lunch on the fifteenth day, I climbed up to the bridge and joined Poulous and Smit leaning over the rail. The mate pointed ahead. 'There you are Sparks, my lad, fine on the starboard bow, the Cape of Eleven Thousand Virgins and the entrance of the Magellan Straits.' Poulous laughed. 'It's called "The Virgins" on the chart.' 'I don't care what it says on the chart, old man, Magellan christened it the Cape of Eleven Thousand Virgins', said Smit. 'That's a hell of a lot of virgins', I broke in. 'I didn't know there were that many around even in his day.' 'Magellan was no Greek, anyway' said Poulous. 'There aren't that number of virgins in the whole of Greece.' 'No, he was a Portuguese, and in my few trips to Lisbon I never found one', said Smit. 'Things must have changed since Magellan's day.'

We passed through the Outer and Inner Narrows, which presented us with no trouble but must have been difficult to traverse in small sailing ships not noted for going to windward. We entered Broad Reach and then anchored about a mile off Punta Arenas. It didn't seem much of a town, mostly wooden houses with tin roofs, but we soon became aware of the Punta Arenas wind. We were there two weeks and it blew steadily every day without fail, although it did sometimes give over for a while in the evening.

When the skipper returned on board, he was full of woe: we would have to discharge the ship ourselves and the harbour authorities wouldn't allow us ashore because we had no quarantine clearance from Rio. Poor little Poulous was heartbroken. 'Pluddy crooks in Rio give me paper, pluddy crooks here say no good, only for ass.' So we set to and discharged the ship with the crew. A barge came alongside with three steel buckets which we dipped in the hatch. The mate rigged the derricks, I drove the winch that lifted the filled bucket out of the hold and Smit drove the winch that took up the weight and then dropped the bucket into the barge. All hands turned to filling the buckets, even little Poulous wielding a shovel. In the steady westerly wind we were almost choked with dust, and I couldn't help recalling the dreams of a young officer in his smart uniform squiring the young lady passengers round the decks in the moonlight. I had travelled a long way, mostly backwards.

I went ashore with Poulous on the last day, expecting to be arrested for breaking quarantine; but no one took the slightest notice of us, and a policeman even helped us tie up the ship's dinghy. I think the real truth was that poor little Poulous just hadn't the money to grease the right palms, and the owner had written in the charter for the crew to discharge the ship anyway. We walked together to the office of a Syrian gentleman who claimed to be the owner's agent, where I left Poulous and went to a bar called the Antarctic Bar. The barman accepted an English pound note as legal tender, less 20 per cent, and I was halfway through my second bottle when Poulous joined me with a face as long as a fiddle. 'These people make an Arab bumboatman look like a preacher,' he complained. 'They almost charge me for the coal we used getting steam on the windlass to lift the hook.' He accepted a beer. 'We go to Rosario, Cape Town and then Japan. Maybe stop at Hong Kong for bunkers.'

Tramp ships, I was learning, had the wandering Jew beaten by a mile. Next day we cleared the Virgins and started plodding up the lines of latitude again. Five days later we had a real shock—the dawn showed long rolled layers of cloud towards the South American coast, and by noon we were to have the worst gale I was ever to experience. The wind was so strong that it flattened the sea, and the poor old *Katerina*, steaming flat out, just remained shuddering in the same hole in the water. You couldn't breathe, walk or talk; we all huddled in the chartroom on the lower bridge. Being a light ship she stood out of the water like the side of a house, and the only possible course was to steam into the wind. I am convinced that she would have blown over if she had got beam on. By 4pm the wind had dropped to a gentle breeze. 'That's what they call a pampero, Sparks', said Smit at supper. 'See all that hay and dust go flying by; must have blown half the state of Argentina out to sea. I thought I saw a gaucho go sailing by, still on his horse and whirling his bolas round his head.' Poulous looked up from his hash. 'Why he do that, Mister Mate—must be pluddy painful.' Smit turned to me. 'The ignorance of the working classes, Sparks!'

The port authorities in Rosario seemed pleased to see us. They positively rushed us under the grain silos, and soon the *Katerina's* holds were being filled with maize from the big adjustable trunks. Unfortunately, in Rosario Smit really ran into trouble. He was an intelligent and well read man, but at times the endless squalor of his life seemed too much for him and he would go on great drinking bouts. On the first day in Rosario he apparently bullied Poulous into giving him a few pesos, and then vanished. Three days later, with the *Katerina* down to her marks with grain, a very worried Poulous came along and said: 'Come ashore with me, Sparks. The mate in plenty trouble, we go get him out'.

'Plenty trouble' was a colossal understatement. We found Smit in the drunk tank, a tiny windowless cell in the yard of the police station, sharing the filthy floor with half a dozen others in the same state of alcoholic collapse. His clothes were gone, even his socks, and he had two black eyes and a nasty festering cut across one cheek. The policeman rolled Smit over with his boot. 'Belong you?' he asked. 'Yes', said Poulous, 'he belong us. Go back to the ship, Sparks, and get some clothes while I give him wash.' When I returned, Poulous had Smith out of the drunk tank and was trying to clean him up with a bucket of water. While Poulous went with the policeman to settle the fine, I got Smit into a shirt and trousers. He seemed more drugged than drunk, but appeared to know me. We took him back to the ship in a horse-drawn Black Maria supplied by the police.

We sailed down the River Plate with Poulous on the fo'c'sle head, me at the wheel, the second mate aft, and the Argentine pilot in charge of the bridge. The pilot's mother had been English, and he was deeply intrigued with the running of the *Katerina*, where the captain acted as first mate and the radio operator as helmsman. 'How in hell does an Englishman finish up on an old tub like this!' he asked. 'I hear your crew are all nationalities.' 'All except Eskimo', I corrected him. 'It's perfectly simple. I was sent here by my company for a coasting trip and I have just stayed. They're not a bad mob to sail with. The mate's a Belgian and has been teaching me navigation, the second mate's a Greek and I'm teaching him English, and I am radio operator-cum unofficial third-mate.' He asked about the food. 'Pretty bloody', I admitted, 'but no worse than a Welsh tramp I was in once.' The pilot laughed. 'Guess they're all pretty much the same these days.' I agreed that tramps were tramps, but that the ancient *Katerina* was, in her rough way, a happy ship—there were no problems of national pride, at least. The pilot then explained that we would have to wait at least three days for the water to be deep enough for us to cross the Martin Garcia Bar. He anchored us and then went ashore.

Slowly Smit pulled himself together. He didn't remember much about his trip ashore, even his drinking companions. Poulous was sure he would recover, though he went on: 'Some of the rotgut they sell in South America would stun an elephant. The first few drinks they sell you are perhaps reasonable liquor, but from then on it could be anything. I had a sailor brought back to my ship once in Santos who just didn't wake up at all in the fo'c'sle. The doctors did an autopsy and found that he had a gut full of paraffin and wood alcohol'. 'Christ, skipper!' I exclaimed. 'How in God's name do you swallow muck like that?' Poulous smiled. 'Remember, Sparks, most of the drifters that man these old ship have nothing—no home or country, and most of them not even a name of their own. They don't go ashore for a drink as you do; they go ashore to drink to forget.'

Four days later we sailed down the Rio de la Plata and out into the South Atlantic on our long slog to Cape Town, 3,720 miles of it. It was a fair-weather passage, and twenty-one days later we saw Table Mountain, complete with tablecloth appearing with the dawn. Smit had fully recovered, my lessons had been resumed and we hadn't seen even a wisp of smoke since leaving South America. The only problem during that voyage was that Poulous had taken on a deck cargo of animal bones for delivery to Hong Kong. As soon as the sun shone on them, millions of minute black flies appeared. They got into everything—ears, nose and hair—and the food was black with them. Life was hellish, and Smit was all for dumping them over the side. 'What in hell's name does a bloody Hong Kong Chink want with animal bones! Got plenty of his ancestors to dig up if he wants them, without dragging them all the way from Rosario', he raged. Then we ran through the doldrums, where short intense downpours of rain killed off all the flies but left a foul stench. The pilot that took us into Cape Town anchored us in Table Bay. 'Can't take you alongside smelling like that. Your bunkers will be sent out in barges', he said. We had all got used to the smell, I suppose, because we were all hurt at this treatment. Smit knew a 'place' there where he was willing to take me if I would pay, because the police fines in Rosario had put his minute salary in hock to the ship for months to come; but it was not to be. We bunkered, loaded stores and sailed in the evening. Go to sea and see the sea was obviously to be my lot.

It took us forty-nine days to get to Hong Kong, but the smell cleared and there was no problem about letting us in. We were put on the buoys, and, while the Chinese coolies were making short order of getting our deck cargo overside into a barge, I thought I would go to the company's office ashore and collect some money. Even there the old *Katerina* was in trouble: the owner had never paid for my valuable services and all the company's overseas offices had been circu- larised to ship me home when I showed up. I signed on the *Hai Ning* that afternoon, and in the evening watched the old

Katerina and her crew of homeless men waddle through the Lyee Moon Pass on her endless voyage. She apparently sailed with a Chinese radio operator, but I never came across her again.

The *Hai Ning* was a smart coaster owned by the Douglas Steamship Company, and operated a regular service—Hong Kong, Swatow, Amoy, Foochow and back to Hong Kong. She had a Chinese crew, and married Australian officers whose wives lived in Hong Kong. She was a smart ship with excellent food, but once again I found myself the outside man. The officers' accommodation was under guard throughout the trip and I had to report the ship's position to the British Navy on Stonecutters Island every four hours. Shipowners were very careful about Chinese pirates getting aboard with the genuine deck passengers and taking over the ship once she reached the sea. Successful pirates would then direct the ship to their own ports, where she and the passengers were looted at leisure. I was on the *Hai Ning* for eight months, but nothing happened at all; perhaps the pirates were put off by the huge service revolver that I had to take with me when I went on watch in the radio cabin.

My next move was to the P&O *Ranchi* as third radio man for the trip back to England. The least said about the *Ranchi* the better. I was now getting rather long in the tooth for a third radio man, and I doubtless failed to give my seniors their due respect. I signed off in East Ham and went on leave.

When my next posting came, I was sent again to Cardiff, and appointed to the SS *Ruckinge*, owned by Constants Ltd and discharging iron ore in Port Talbot. The *Ruckinge* was a new type of ship to me, being what was known as a 'weekly boat'. The owners paid you 2s 6d a day to supply your own food, and the crew were paid each week. She was only just big enough to need radio, and was on a regular run—Bristol Channel to France with coal, and then down to Santander or Bilbao in Spain to load iron ore for the steelworks of Guest, Keen & Nettlefold in Port Talbot. I had two surprises in store—she was the smallest ship I was ever to sail in—an outsize coaster of 1,742 tons built in 1923—and the accommodation was the best. The whole of the rooms on the lower bridge were turned over to radio—a comfortable cabin and a reasonably sized radio room. Being a local ship, she was again crewed by Welshmen, but they were a very different crowd from the gang on the *Alban*. Captain Lloyd came from Cross Keys and was a grand old man who had spent years in the Bristol Channel and knew it like the back of his hand. The first mate was an elderly man who had fallen on hard times; he had been captain of his own ship for years until his owners had gone into liquidation. The second mate was another casualty of the shipping slump, who had been a first mate. The bosun, Zaleck, was a Greek who had sailed with Captain Lloyd for years, and the four sailors were his nephews. The chief engineer came from Bristol and brought with him his own black gang of Arabs, who had also sailed with him for a long time. The chief steward and cook was an important man in a 'weekly' boat, since he did the catering and cooking for the officers. The rest of the crew did their own cooking, and, when we were loading the coal or discharging the iron ore, they went home. I found the strangest thing about the *Ruckinge* was that I was the only single man on board; even the steward's boy, a lad of eighteen, was the proud father of two sons in a terraced house in Splott, near the Cardiff Docks. As I was unpacking my case, Captain Lloyd came into the cabin and settled himself in my chair. 'Sparks, I want to tell you about the way we run these weekly boats. You have picked up a little, I expect, but I would like to fill it in. The trip takes about fourteen days, and, as we pay the men at the end of each trip, it would be a great help to me if you would act as the ship's clerk.' He held up his hands and I could see that they were crippled with rheumatism. 'I'll check 'em for you and show you what to do for a while, but writing is not too easy for me. With the two mates on watch and watch, and spending most of our time in congested waters, I don't get much spare time.' 'I will most certainly do it, sir', I replied. 'There won't be much for me to do except collect your

K

weather for the coastal waters.' The skipper nodded.

While he was telling me how the weekly articles operated, the chief engineer popped his head through the door. The skipper laughed. 'Come in, chief, Sparks has taken on my work; if he will now take on yours, we shall all be happy'. The chief, a man in his late sixties, explained his problem. 'My firemen and the trimmers are Arabs that have lived in the Bristol Channel for years. They are all married to white women and all have families. Will you write their letters for them and look after their bankbooks? They like to put away a little each trip in the Post Office.' I agreed that this seemed no real problem. 'Just take so much out of their wages, they'll tell you how much', the chief continued. 'Most of their wives are not exactly the type to be trusted to save money, as you'll find when you meet them.' The chief explained that he and the second engineer were on watch and watch like the mates, so they didn't have time to look after that sort of thing. I asked the captain about the deck crew. Captain Lloyd laughed. 'Old Zaleck, the bosun, runs them entirely on his own. He is a kind of headman for the Greek sailors in this area. He, too, is married, with two sons, but he won't have them at sea with him. Claims they undermine his position. He details who stays to help the ship being moved under the tips and sets the watches.' He went on to say that it was the easiest way to run the ship, as some of the sailors had only a rudimentary command of English.

The steward was my next visitor. Cliff and I were to become good friends. He had been a deep-sea cook before joining the *Ruckinge*, and had married a Cardiff girl. He now had three children and was the same age as I was. The crew of the *Ruckinge* seemed to have combined seagoing with marriage pretty successfully. 'The Old Man tells me you have taken on the ship's clerical work', said Cliff, after he had introduced himself. 'If you will give me the 2s 6d a day you draw for each of us at the end of the trip, I can buy provisions for the next one.' I agreed to do this. 'You can keep your pay and feed yourself if you like.' I laughed and declined. 'Had one crazy bugger that did some years ago. He claimed that he could do it cheaper than I could. In two months he had the whole of the lower bridge looking like a ships' chandler's store. He even peeled and cooked his own potatoes, and carried it all into the saloon to eat.' I repeated that I did not intend to cook for myself, then asked what happened about the crew's food if we were delayed. 'That's the real problem in weekly boats', replied Cliff. 'I feed them out of my reserve stores and then try and claim the money back. That's where you can help, Sparks.'

The next day the *Ruckinge* moved along the coast to Penarth to load coal for Nantes. It was the Indian coast again, but without the heat and with rain to damp the dust down. I found that the best plan was to go into digs in Cardiff during loading and discharging, as the ship wasn't a very pleasant place to live in. Within a few days of leaving Penarth, we were under the grabs discharging in Nantes. The ship was soon empty, and then we sailed down the Bay of Biscay to Santander to load iron ore for Port Talbot. Iron ore has little to recommend it as a cargo, except that it isn't as dirty as coal, and the ship was loaded down to her marks with the holds only partly filled. The cargo lowered the centre of gravity and made the ship roll badly in a beam sea. We had quite a dusting as we sailed north across the Bay with a south-westerly gale, and I had to jam myself in the bunk to stay in it at all.

At Santander I had my first experience of reading and writing other people's letters. They were hardly literary gems, but the firemen were deeply interested in their families, and enquiries about their health and doings made up the bulk of their replies. I found that old Zaleck, too, was a customer. He brought me a long letter from his wife, mostly a complaint about his going to sea and leaving her without money. 'You tell bloody woman, she always write "Zaleck, Zaleck, send me money". Why don't she go to workhouse if she so bloody poor? I send her nothing.' I wrote and told Mrs Zaleck about Mr Zaleck's financial problems, and suggested that she hang on until our return to Port Talbot. The skipper was highly amused. 'That old Greek crook owns a row of houses in Barry, and could buy and sell you and me, Sparks.' I was to find this was true. Zaleck was making a small levy on each of his nephews who came and went on deck in the *Ruckinge*. The old rascal even tackled me about subtracting his levy from the sailors before I paid them—I suppose today we would call it streamlining the operation. 'Zaleck, you old crook, I can't do that.' He protested. 'Why no can't do? Plenty officers at sea today pay shipowner or maybe captain leetle money each month for job on sheep.' The trouble was that the old man was telling the truth. He carried on. 'These nephews I have, they no money. Zaleck feed them. Why you no pay me that grub money direct? Zaleck always has plenty trouble to get grub money on payday.' It was only logic but hardly likely to make the shipping master happy.

I asked Cliff about Zaleck feeding the sailors. 'Yes, that's true all right; he buys half a dozen sheeps' heads and boils them up in turn. Come down to the galley and have a look.' The galley range was covered with cooking pots, including a large black saucepan whose lid Cliff lifted with a long spoon. Inside was a complete sheep's head and, from the scummy water, a bright blue eye gazed stonily at me. 'That's Zaleck's soup', explained Cliff. 'That's all they have from start to finish; they drink it down with bread and wash away the taste with gipsy tea.' He pointed to a paint tin bubbling away full of dark liquid.

We arrived in Port Talbot, the skipper went ashore for the money, then I paid off the crew and balanced the ship's books. The three firemen—Jebel Hawk, Abdul Aziz and Said Mohamed—each wanted money put in their Post Office books, which was done; and, accompanied by most of the crew, I set off to Cardiff in the bus. We seemed to have no colour problems in the *Ruckinge*: Jebel Hawk sat beside me in the bus and talked about the new house he wanted to buy, while Cliff and the second mate spent the journey trying to explain football to Abdul Aziz. The two Arabs came from Aden, and, although they could neither read or write English, their grasp of the monetary system was first-class. They knew to a penny what wages were due to them, and what they had in the Post Office.

For ôver a year we pottered to and fro, visiting most of the ports in Northern France—Nantes, St Nazaire, La Pallice, St Malo, and, my favourite spot, La Rochelle, and then going down the Bay to either Santander or Bilbao for iron ore. On one trip we had to put Jebel Hawk ashore in St Nazaire with appendicitis, and I wrote to his wife and told her what had happened. Cliff brought her into the radio room when we got to Port Talbot. She was a pleasant woman and reasonably well dressed, and had come to collect Jebel's wages. Perhaps I wasn't as kind as I should have been, because she turned on me after I had handed her the money. 'You don't think much of me being married to an Arab, do you?' she asked. I denied having any feelings about it one way or the other. I knew Jebel and I liked him. 'One thing about being married to an Arab fireman, he doesn't piss all his money up the wall. You should see some of the poor cows in our street that are married to white firemen. A big booze-up when he signs on and gets a month's advance, then he goes to sea in the clothes he stands in and leaves her an allotment note. After two months the poor bitch finds he's jumped ship somewhere, and then Christ knows when she will see him again. Only thing she can do is to go on the batter if she's young enough.' I handed her Jebel's Post Office book without comment; this was an aspect of life that I didn't know much about.

In St Nazaire we had filled Jebel's place with a real gypsy of the sea. Captain Lloyd sent me ashore to the agent's office to collect him, and I found him in a tiny prison cell that smelled strongly of urine and Caporal cigarettes. The police had picked him up in the docks, and he claimed to be a Maltese. His lower jaw was displaced sideways so that his teeth didn't meet. He had nothing but some dungarees the police had given him. As we walked back to the *Ruckinge*, stopping at the odd bistro and having a few pastis, he told me some of his story. Malt, as we called him, spoke perfect English with a strong American accent. He had originally shipped as a fireman on a Turkish tramp, though he did not name the port of departure. The food was dreadful, and he made several attempts to desert; but it hadn't been easy, for in the smaller ports in the Mediterranean the Turkish captain had paid the local chief of police to arrest all the firemen and keep them in gaol until sailing day. Eventually the ship had loaded for Rio de Janeiro, where he had absconded. He had remained under cover in a park in Rio until she sailed and then had given himself up. The Brazilian police put him aboard a French ship, which was no better than the Turk, but Malt jumped ship in New York and vanished into the multi-racial population of lower New York.

He found a job as a clothes presser with an Armenian tailor and, after sleeping in the shop storeroom for a few weeks, branched out and took a room in a boarding house. He lived in New York for two years. I heard this part of the story in the radio room one day. 'Sparks, then I got myself too smart and started looking for a girl. I didn't have to look far; in the next room to mine was an oldish tart who dressed young and worked in a flower shop. I took her out a couple of times and, Sparks, was that old gal hungry for a man? In no time I was two blocks and she was talking of marriage.' I interrupted. 'Come off it, Malt. What about that bloody twisted mug of yours? She didn't want that to admire for the rest of her life.' 'Sparks, boy, she was so godammed hungry she would even take that on, for wedding bells—wanted it steady with her corsets off I figured. I tried to explain that there was a big difference between helping her out and being stuck with it for all time, so she went straight down to the precinct house and reported me as an illegal immigrant. They didn't know where to deport me to, so they shoved me aboard a Greek that was short of a fireman, and the old game started all over again.'

Malt kept me interested for hours with his stories of ships that sailed under what we now call 'flags of convenience'.

After he had been with us for about six weeks, we had a break in the usual routine—we were sent to Bordeaux for a load of pitprops and then back to Newport. When sailing day came, Malt was missing. I visited the police and reported him missing, but he had vanished for good and Jebel, recovered from his operation, rejoined us in Port Talbot. There were changes in the air. The Spanish Civil War was now in full fling and fortunes were being made by shipowners who would send their ships down to Spain. So we were not surprised when Captain Lloyd came aboard with some real news. The *Ruckinge* had been sold to Watts Watts Co and our new name was to be the *Mortlake*. There were to be no changes in the ship's complement, but we were going on the Spanish run. Potato Jones and his *Sevon Seas Spray* were now national heroes, so perhaps we would make the headlines with the old *Mortlake*. What interested me most was that our pay was to be doubled while we were on the Spanish Coast and in danger of being bombed.

We went to Antwerp and loaded a cargo of wooden cases labelled 'Tinned Milk—Made in Switzerland'. I never saw one opened, so I can only assume they were what they claimed to be. We sailed for Gibraltar to pick up our Non-Intervention Observer—non-intervention being a Government device to ensure that no shipowner was actively engaged in helping either side in the Civil War. The observer's job was to watch the cargo being discharged, and ensure that it contained no war material. The observers were drawn from all walks of life from various countries, but were mostly retired army and navy characters, though it was reported that one ship under the Swiss flag had an observer from the Salvation Army. They had a hopeless task, for the ships were fully loaded when they joined them and were discharged by Spanish dockers in Spanish ports. They never knew what the ship was actually carrying and, as they were not real sailors, all hands took a delight in hoodwinking them. I once watched a purple faced ex-British army major trying to persuade some Spanish dockers to break open a case on the dock at Barcelona; they just shrugged their shoulders while he had apoplexy, and in the argument the case vanished.

The observer we picked up in Gibraltar was from the Irish Free State. He claimed to have a master's ticket, but I believe this was untrue from later conversations I had with him. I think he had served his time in the Head Line and had a second mate's ticket. Tall, thin and dark, Paddy was the most emotional person in the world. He was already seated at the saloon teatable when I came in and Captain Lloyd introduced me. After listening to my conventional remarks for a minute, he broke into a towering rage. 'They told me at the Non-Intervention Office that this was a Welsh ship, and now I find a cursed Englishman sitting down at the same table. I'd sooner feed with pigs in a trough than with the cursed bastard of a Black and Tan.' I can see dear old Captain Lloyd now, thumping his deformed hands down on each side of his plate. 'This ship is British', he said quietly. 'We have Welshmen, Englishmen, Arabs and Greeks', and with a laugh at the chief, 'even a Bristolian. You can sail with us or take your hate back ashore, I don't care. If you stay, you'll keep your bloody politics out of my saloon. We have all sailed together for a long time and are good friends, and I won't have any of this Ireland-for-ever crap.' Paddy blinked twice. 'All right, captain; if dat's de way of things, 'tis a pity, but I'll stay.'

As the *Mortlake* sailed along the Spanish Coast, Paddy and I became friendly; I was the only one, anyway, with any free time to talk to him. He told me his story and it explained his bitter hatred of 'de English'. He had been mixed up with Sir Roger Casement's followers during World War I and had been in command of a tug smuggling German arms into Ireland. He used to sneak along the French coast, mostly in the dark, and then nip across to Southern Ireland and unload the cargo. Paddy said he made three trips before he was caught. He was convinced that he had been betrayed, and he probably was, because he was easing very quietly into a deserted bay in the far west of Ireland one black night when suddenly a searchlight jumped out of the dark and within minutes a

British destroyer was alongside him. Paddy served four years in a British prison, nursing his hate. I couldn't find out what he had been doing since his discharge from prison, but he hadn't been at sea. Cliff, who had heard the story, too, thought he might have been hunting down the informer.

When we docked in Barcelona, however, we found out what he had been doing—and that was boozing. Paddy arranged for a ships' chandler to bring aboard a barrel of what he called 'Creme de Christo', which tasted like cheap port wine. Paddy supped away at this all day and most of the night, and in two days he was in a pitiable state. The cargo was discharged at high speed, but poor Paddy didn't even look at it. There was no cabin for him and his official bunk was the saloon settee, but he took the cushion off my settee and slept on the vegetable locker right alongside his barrel.

The port of Barcelona was a real picture. The world was making loud noises about not intervening in the Spanish Civil War, but the money boys weren't listening. Anything that would float was going into the anti-Franco ports loaded with cases labelled food. Some arrived with top cargoes of fruit for the starving populace, but under the fruit were yet more cases of tinned milk. Some of the ships flew a Non-Intervention flag and carried an official observer, some were just painted black, without a name or a port of registry. Cliff and I had several nights ashore at the Hotel Europa in the Rue Rambler, and it was an exciting business. Twice volleys of shots burst out in the streets, where another Carlist had been rooted out. There seemed to be no shortage of booze, and the place was full of the crews of blockade-runners spending freely. When we were empty, the ship was moved to Alicante, where we loaded a full cargo of oranges.

According to the rules, Non-Intervention Observers were not allowed to leave the ship, but these rules didn't apply to Paddy. His Creme de Christo had been finished on the trip down to Alicante, and, within two days, in an appalling state, he vanished ashore. On the day before sailing a Spanish policeman and an interpreter came aboard, and as everybody in authority was busy, they were passed on to me. They had arrested Paddy the night before, asleep in a flowerbed in the City Park, and, from studying his papers, knew who he was and what ship he was off. Would I come and collect the body? Paddy, who was asleep in a small white cell, was far from happy at being awakened to return to the *Mortlake*, especially by one of the cursed English. The patience of the police was about exhausted by now; they slung him into a horse-drawn Black Maria and, with me on the box, returned the body to the *Mortlake*. None too gently Paddy was pulled up the gangway and dropped on the deck. Later Zaleck played the deck hose on him, and then got the sailors to throw him on the vegetable locker, since he stank of booze and vomit and Captain Lloyd refused to have him back in the saloon. The cargo of oranges was for Antwerp, but we put Paddy into the Non-Intervention launch in the outer harbour at Gib and proceeded on our way. No one saw or heard of him again. He was the victim of his own hates, but by his reasoning had been fighting for his country, and, when caught, had been treated like a criminal instead of a prisoner of war.

In Antwerp we again loaded cases of milk and set off for Barcelona. Again we picked up a Non-Intervention Observer in Gibraltar, and in a short time wished that we had Paddy back, with all his problems. The new one was a retired army major whose first action on joining was to refuse to sleep on the saloon settee. 'I am an ex-officer and demand officer's accommodation and status aboard this ship', he stated loudly. He was a long lean man who emphasised all his statements by banging a short stick against his leg. He also had bright blue eyes and a scrubby little moustache—a perfect carica-ture of an ex-army officer. Dear old Captain Lloyd was no match for him at all. It was explained that there wasn't a spare cabin as we were only an outsize coaster. The major then stated that he would inspect what accommodation there was, and muttered darkly about 'some of the juniors doubling up'. The whole situation was getting tense when suddenly the old chief mate flew off the handle. A quiet patient man,

I had never seen him angry before. 'You heard what the captain said; there is no separate cabin for you. Shall I chuck the bastard over the side, sir? He's stinking the whole ship up.' The major piped down right away and agreed that he would sleep in the saloon. 'What happened to the mate?' I asked Cliff later. 'That outburst wasn't like him at all, completely out of character.' Cliff replied: 'He was the skipper of a trooper during the war, and had a hell of a row with the OC troops which ended in the owner's office with the Old Lad losing his command. An army uniform just makes him see red, always has done since I've known him.' 'The Army' as the major was called on board, must have found life a dreary business. He was anti-everything and eventually no one wanted to talk to him; even the galley boy wouldn't pass the time of day.

We found that the war was going badly for the Republicans in Barcelona. Several blockade-runners had been damaged at sea, and several that had been sunk in the docks during air raids were sitting on the bottom. Cliff and I set out for the Europa again, but it was a changed place. Several of the streets around had been damaged by bombs and the happy-go-lucky blockade-running crews were much quieter. Money, booze and food were all in short supply. Cliff and I were even handed some paper money printed by the Europa itself as change for a pound note, each piece of paper being worth so much in booze. One evening I had a long chat with a German prostitute who had been in great demand on our last visit, but her business, too, had fallen off. She was a German Jewess who had built up a hairdresser's business with her husband in Barcelona, but, soon after the war started, the husband had been dragged out into the street and shot by a gang of youths who thought he was a German Fascist. She had carried on for a while, but then the shop had been bombed and two of her children killed; and she now lived in a cellar under the ruins of the shop with her sole remaining child. 'My husband and I left Germany to get away from the Fascists and give our children a chance to live, and this is the result.' Cliff brought her some tinned food ashore the next night, but we both refused her offer to pay in the only way she could. Passion in a bombed-out cellar with a child watching didn't appeal to either of us.

There were several air raids on Barcelona, and we got used to going back to the ship in the dense haze of dust that always seemed to hang over the city after a raid. They were pretty small compared with those of World War II, but it was the first time we had seen a fallen house surrounded by dozens of helpless people who knew that friends and acquaintances were hopelessly buried underneath. Perhaps it made us appreciate our double pay. The Barcelona docks received quite a pasting one night and the *Mortlake* received several holes in the funnel from shrapnel, but they were to be our only war scars. We sailed from Barcelona to Antwerp again, and three times on our way down to Gibraltar were closely inspected by Franco aircraft; they were floatplanes and seemed interested mainly in the ship's name. The Non-Intervention flag didn't seem to impress them too much. We put our private Army ashore in Gibraltar, and Captain Lloyd took me ashore with him so that I could return to the ship with some money to buy food. When he returned, he had some real news—we were going back to the Bristol Channel again. Everyone was relieved, except perhaps some of Zaleck's nephews, who only wanted the double pay; and I had a couple of busy hours writing all the 'I'll soon be home' letters. Old Zaleck didn't dictate his. 'Just tell bloody woman, Zaleck come home and find what she done with his bloody money.'

On the way home Captain Lloyd came into the radio cabin one day, settled down and fired up his pipe. 'We have been together a long time as ships go, Sparks, and I am going to give you a piece of my mind. It's time you got ashore and found yourself a proper job. There is nothing in the sea for a radio operator. One day, after years and years of hungry gutted tramps, someone in the radio company may like the colour of your hair or, more likely, the colour of your money, and you will be promoted to what the chaps call a first-class ship. Somewhere along the line you'll get married—if I know you, you will probably have to—and then you will be too poor to buy yourself a pint. You will have some money coming to you from this Spanish Civil War pay, so go home and look around.'

After Captain Lloyd had gone, I talked it over with Cliff and then with the chief; I even talked with old Zaleck. They all gave me the same advice—if you want to amount to anything, pack it up—but perhaps old Zaleck expressed himself best. 'Sparks, I been at sea fifty year, no bloody good. Sparksmen like bloody firemen, different on every ship. You marry, how can watch bloody woman at sea? You finish like Zaleck —broke old man all time.'

I had heard that aircraft carried radio operators, and I decided to try for that. I left the old *Mortlake* under the coal tips in Barry—she was the happiest ship I had ever sailed in—and faced life ashore, something I had never done since I had grown up. After I left, the ship was to have yet another owner, J. A. Billmeir & Co, who renamed her *Stanlake*. She was sunk by an E-boat in April 1943, 12 miles off the Lizard, in water through which she had often struggled against easterly gales to reach the Bristol Channel.

CHAPTER EIGHT

Postscript

IN 1935 I started my flying career, which carried on until 1941. The war was on, but with glasses I was unacceptable to the RAF, even with an Air Radio Operator's licence and a Navigator's licence. I was told very firmly that they wouldn't even have me as a truck driver. All my problems were solved, however, in a short letter from His Majesty's Government: I was to report to the Merchant Navy Shipping Pool in Cardiff at once. There I was informed that I was to go back to sea again, a thought that filled me with a gloom lightened somewhat by finding the chief engineer and the second mate of the *Mortlake* sitting quietly in one corner of the waiting room. We adjourned to the nearest pub and started on the business of 'Do you remember old so and so?' The chief was now on a deep-sea cargo boat, but the second mate was the captain of a coaster, having given up the deep sea for an occasional night at home. 'Nice for the kids to recognise their father', was his way of putting it. 'Any idea what you are going to get, Sparks?' asked the chief. I said that I hadn't a clue, since I hadn't seen a ship for six years. 'There won't be any problem of finding you one', laughed the chief. 'All the long voyage ships carry three radio men now.' He was right. On my returning to the Pool at closing time, the clerk called me over. 'Got a ship for you. Join her at Newport in the morning', and he handed me some papers across the desk. I showed the papers to the chief. 'Never heard of her', he said, and passed them to the second mate, who took one look and burst into laughter. 'Trust you, Sparks. You've hit the jackpot. The *Lady Wolmer* is built of concrete and reputed to be the first of a long line; she'll sink like a bloody stone if she even touches a quay wall.'

The next day I found the *Lady Wolmer* in Newport, and she was, as the second mate had said, a ferro-concrete coaster of 1,883 gross tons, built like a house by W. & C. French Ltd of Newport. She had just been floated out of her drydock and tied to the dock wall, and this was her maiden voyage. The captain was called Bobby behind his back by all hands, and was a very decent old chap from the Isle of Magee. He became my firm friend when he found I was an expert ship's clerk on weekly boats. The chief engineer was a Scotsman who had been working in the diamond mines in South Africa and had been ashore longer than me. The second engineer was a Dutch Javanese who had just escaped the Japs and by devious routes had got to England. The *Lady Wolmer* was a motorship with an opposed piston diesel that the chief claimed had been removed from a Glasgow Museum. The cook steward was a coloured man from Bristol, and both the first and second officers were retired shipmasters who had returned to sea because of the war.

It was a mixed atmosphere at breakfast the next morning, when we were to make our first passage from Newport to Barry to load coal for Devonport dockyard: Bobby was convinced everything would be all right, the chief that his opposed pistons would lock solid and the two master mariners that she would sink like a stone in Newport Roads. I was detailed to work the Aldis signalling lamp and try to keep out of the sailors' way, as the second mate put it. At first all went well, though the chief's museum reject made a hell of a thumping noise, and the gunners scared us all with a few practice rounds. Then, going through the dock gates in Barry, we hit the wall. A steel ship would not even have noticed it, but the *Lady Wolmer* gave a horrible crumbling sound. The dock pilot was amazed, not knowing he was handling the first of a long line of concrete coasters. The ship was pushed away into the corner of the dock and we examined the damage: a large section of concrete had crumbled away on one side and left the steel reinforcing rods open to the air. The hole was cemented up, and then the dock authorities moved us under the coal tips as gently as though the ship had been made of eggshells.

For eight months we pottered round the coast with coal, but we were continually being held up for repairs to the concrete when we touched a dock wall. 'Wonder they don't sign on a gang of building workers instead of sailors', said one of the crew. After a disastrous trip through the Manchester Ship Canal, we were sent back to Newport. There a letter from the Shipping Pool told me that I had been released to RAF Ferry Command as a radio operator; my pre-war licences had been found and use was to be made of them. I left the *Lady Wolmer* in the corner of the dock in Newport, and for the second time I gave up the sea, this time for good. Two years later I was to meet Bobby again. He was in Montreal awaiting a brand new ship. 'The economics of the *Lady Wolmer* were wrong', he said over a beer. 'They hadn't figured out how long it would take the concrete to set after a repair. She's still bumping around, I believe.' I never heard of her again.